*"If you want an honest and c[...] Jesus, this book offers wisc[...] Tommy's authentic accou[...] along with clear leading fror[...] informative toolkit to dip in and out of throughout life. We have witnessed Tommy not only give life-changing teachings and watched his heart for encouraging others pour out onto the pages of this book. This is a book that leads us into a deeper understanding of the authority and power given to us, whilst challenging the reader to influence their sphere well."*
**Stephen and Allison Crawford, Co-Founders, Coaching4Christ**

"For as long as I have known Tommy he has been an encourager of those around him. This book reflects his heart to encourage Christians in leadership roles. He draws on his extensive experience: first, his experience of being a child of God, and then of serving and consulting with many different organisations and churches. This book is accessible and practical as well as inspiring and encouraging. I heartily recommend it to anyone who finds themselves in with leadership responsibilities in the church and in the workplace."
**Rev John Alderdice, Methodist Minister and Arrow Leadership Director**

*"Tommy Stewart carries a remarkable gift of encouraging and equipping people across a wide range of organisations, ministries and churches, nationally and internationally. To be around Tommy is to be in the company of someone who has a passion for living and leading like Jesus and to be impacted by the overflow of his heart, wisdom and experience in leadership. He gives his time and heart like Jesus. This first book by Tommy is not only to be read, but to be studied, prayed, applied and shared. Thank you, Tommy, for inspiring us to live and lead like Jesus."*
**Fergus McMorrow, Director, Divine Healing Ministries**

*"Tommy has been a trusted friend to me at both a personal and ministry level for many years. His encouragement and teaching of Christian leaders is something which I have been privileged to experience on both national and international platforms. After reading 'Live and Lead Like Jesus', I am challenged and motivated to lead at a higher level. I know this book will be a great resource for Christian leaders throughout the world."*
**Ronnie Dawson. Founder/Director, Drop Inn Ministries**

*"This is a valuable working manual for any leader who seeks to grow in identity, insight and impact. Drawing from his years of considerable experience championing other leaders both locally and globally, Tommy provides practical tools for development and inspires the reader to be proactive to live and lead like Jesus – something we should all aspire to!"*
**Alyson and Hugh Reid, Vineyard Pastors**

*"Sometimes the simplest things are the hardest things to get right. We can make the simplest things more complicated than they ever need to be. Tommy has managed to break down how to live and lead like Jesus in a way that everyone can follow. As you journey through your identity, your inspiration, your impact, and your influence, you will learn simple truths. The challenge will be to not over complicate it as you put it into practice."*
**Catherine Little, Bible Society General Secretary**

*"Tommy Stewart has presented a comprehensive and compelling treatise on life and leadership in family, church, workplace and community, using the life and example of Jesus as a measure. Adoption of Jesus as an*

*example to follow in all of life's interactions is an obvious consequence of acceptance of His identity and His Lordship over all. The pathway described inevitably is a recipe for spiritual success while perhaps not mapping onto the priorities taught by society in general. Nevertheless, there is a timelessness implicit in the methods described. Faith in our Redeemer leads to a fundamental change in identity that builds and is empowered by the Spirit. Inspiration obtained from the Lord leads to a developing ability to share with others and thereby pass on that divine inspiration. Living the Spirit-directed and empowered life, impacts individuals, organisations, communities and ultimately nations. How the world is crying out for such at moment. The influence so obtained can thus have a transforming effect which reaches from our close families and friends to national and indeed international scenes. This is the raw material of revival and rests on the power of God working through ordinary people with extraordinary power and vision. This book describes in intimate detail how this can happen and we all need to read its message."*
**Emeritus Professor Chris Shaw, Queens University**

I have experienced first-hand the depth of Tommy's wisdom and experience around leadership, so I am delighted that he has finally put pen to paper to share his insights. This book will take you on the most insightful journey of discovering what it means to lead like Jesus and become the leader you are called to be. Whatever your stage of leadership, this is a must read. I know this book will become an essential read for every member of my team in the years to come.
**Suzi McLean, National Director Youth for Christ**

# LIVE & LEAD LIKE JESUS

Putting Jesus first in the workplace, community and the church.

**TOMMY STEWART**

Copyright ©2021 Tommy Stewart

The moral right of the author has been asserted.

Apart from any fair dealing for the purposes of research or private study, or criticism or review, as permitted under Copyright, Deign and Patents Act 1998, this publication may only be reproduced, stored or transmitted, in any form or by any means, with prior permission in writing of the publishers, or in any case of the reprographic reproduction in accordance with the terms of licences issued by the Copyright Licensing Agency. Enquiries concerning reproduction outside these terms should be sent to the publishers

Issachar Global Publishing

PO Box 38082

London

SW19 1YQ

UK

www.issacharglobal.com

All Scripture quotations are taken from the Holy Bible, New International Version*. Copyright © 1979, 2011 by Biblica Inc. Used by permission of Zondervan.

**ISBN:** 9798528727349

All rights reserved worldwide.

## Thanks

I would like to express my thanks to God for the grace, wisdom and favour HE has bestowed upon me and express my gratitude to my wife, Roberta, for always believing in me, even when I didn't believe in myself.

Special thanks also go to the trustees and leadership team of 'Christians Who Lead' and to Matt Bird for enabling the dream of writing a book to become a reality.

# Contents

## Introduction

## Section 1: Identity

Chapter 1      Identity Formed
Chapter 2      Identity Transformed
Chapter 3      Identity Empowered

## Section 2: Inspiration

Chapter 4      Being Inspired
Chapter 5      Staying Inspired
Chapter 6      Inspiring Others

## Section 3: Impact

Chapter 7      Impacting People
Chapter 8      Impacting Organisations
Chapter 9      Impacting Communities

## Section 4: Influence

Chapter 10      Growing Influence
Chapter 11      Stewarding Influence
Chapter 12      Maximising Influence

TOMMY STEWART

# Foreword

Tommy Stewart has been a valued friend and encourager in my life since we met in 2019. I have enormous respect for him and his ministry with Christian organisations across the world. Tommy is a humble soul with so many gifts and a willingness to share with abundance when doors open and new paths emerge. His passion for the empowerment of individuals in Kingdom Service is inspirational. Adopting a strategic approach, beginning with the end in mind and creating the road map for the journey, is evident in his engagement with others.

In this his first book, he reflects on the life journey that he has been on and shares simple but profound personal experiences that will resonate with every reader. Few in this world have walked a totally smooth path in life. If life was simply a 'walk in the park' we would never develop strength in our faith. It is only when we reflect on our journey that we realise that 'the bumps on the road are the rocks that we climb on'. We are beautifully reminded by Tommy that, if we erase all the mistakes/encounters/tough times from our past, we erase all the wisdom of our present. To claim God's promises, we need to reflect, celebrate the lessons and release the disappointments, remembering that we are forgiven, protected and empowered for the onward journey.

As I read the book, I was drawn back to a model that challenged me personally and I now use it when working with leaders at all stages in their life journey: the 'Pygmalion effect'. Our beliefs about others influences our actions towards others; that impacts others' beliefs about themselves causing others' actions towards us; reinforcing our beliefs about others ... and so the cycle begins again! Unless we are willing to break the cycle by challenging our beliefs about others, the loop continues and forward movement is not possible. As we journey through each chapter in Tommy's book, the words encourage us to persevere, reflect on God's word, think prayerfully and then move into action. We must achieve the private victory in order to move to public victory: 'seek first to understand and then be understood'. Then, and only then, will the cycle be broken and upward/empowering movement achieved no matter where are on our life journey!

A final thought ... Tommy's words are a timely reminder to stop shrinking to fit places we've outgrown and realise that our biggest asset is our mindset based on God's promises that He is with us each step of the way. Creating the 'river that flows' rather than a 'reservoir that sits still' must be our mission in life. This book provides a sound foundation for using reflection to move to action. Romans 11:29 says 'for the gifts and calling of God are irrevocable' and Ephesians 2:10 'you can choose to walk in them'. How many of us are missing the calling to walk as we are equipped?

I trust that all who immerse themselves in 'Live and Lead Like Jesus' will be truly blessed, refreshed and empowered to use their gifts as 'champions for the Kingdom'!

**Audrey Curry,** *Senior Leadership Team, Stranmillis University College*

LIVE & LEAD LIKE JESUS

TOMMY STEWART

# Introduction

'The world needs more leaders like Jesus' is a statement I have heard many times over the course of my life, work and ministry. But what does that really mean? What would it look like to led like Jesus? What would the result be?

I was born in the 1960s in a rural village in Northern Ireland, the first and only child in my family. Years previously, my mother had been told that she was barren and that she had an inoperable brain tumour. Following a miracle, the doctors found that the tumour had disappeared and it later became evident that her barrenness had, too. From an early age I had a sense that God had a purpose for my life, as a result, although I had no idea what that was! I had no idea that God had an even greater future planned for me beyond my parents' dreams.

My childhood images of leadership came through the lens of church and civic leaders. The church minister was held in high regard in the local community and was someone to be looked up to and respected.

Separate from that, the prominent leadership figures on my radar were community and civic leaders, who appeared on the daily news talking about 'The Troubles' that raged across Northern Ireland from 1969 – 1994. As a 'Child of The Troubles', I saw religion and politics somehow inextricably linked, yet separate pillars of leadership that shaped a generation.

During those days of struggle, I am thankful that God raised several people up in my life who, for me, truly knew what it meant to live and lead like Jesus. Much of what I learned in those early years about 'Jesus-centred leadership' can be attributed to a few Godly men and women who, without fanfare or stage, helped to shape my life as a young man who had come to faith in Jesus on a cold winter's night back in 1971. In these role models I saw traits and characteristics that I trust I now radiate in my own life and leadership

Life's circumstances and challenges, of which I will share more, have also shaped my understanding of leadership and form the basis for this book. I am who I am. A working-class 'Child of The Troubles', who encountered the love of Jesus and has set out on a lifelong journey of understanding more about who I am, what God's purpose is for my life and how my life can impact and influence others.

In writing 'Live and Lead Like Jesus', it is my hope that the book and the resources associated with it will help you live and lead more like Jesus in the workplace, the community and the Church.

# Section 1 : Identity

*How we see ourselves in relation to others within society has a direct impact on our identity.*

# Chapter 1
# **Identity Formed**

Understanding how we have become who we are is essential to understanding how we live and lead each day.

It is my firm belief that the shaping and development of our identity impacts how we shape and develop the lives of our children, work colleagues and those we seek to lead.

In this foundational chapter, I want to set out how our identity, up to this point, has been shaped. The '12 Identity Shapers' I discuss are events that I believe will have had some degree of influence on how your identity has been shaped, and that of everyone you will meet or lead.

Understanding how our identity has been shaped, as well as those we lead, helps us recognise the unique set of circumstances that makes us different from each other. It also helps us appreciate the need to emulate God's grace to everyone we meet.

I grew up in an environment and time that significantly impacted who I became as a young man. It also affected how I expressed my emotions. Your journey may have been very different or similar to mine. I trust that as we explore the '12 Identity Shapers', you come to see how context, community culture and context have shaped your identity and how your identity impacts how you live and lead today.

## Context

Each of us has grown up and lived in a different context. I grew up in a working-class family in Northern Ireland in the 1970s; I had no siblings, and my parents could not work due to serious health issues. It was a time of conflict and trouble in our nation when soldiers patrolled the streets with people dying daily through shootings or bomb attacks. Yet amid these circumstances, I grew up in a home shaped by faith and love and a determination to believe, even when everything else seemed to be falling apart.

Over the years, I have come to believe that the context of our upbringing provides us with the first three of the '12 Identify Shapers'.

## Identity Shaper 1: Family
**Our most informative years are shaped by those closest to us**

Due to the challenges faced by my parents, I grew up in a home where my mother and father were at home most of the time. As a result, both had a significant role in shaping my identity. In addition, my paternal grandmother lived with us; she played a crucial part in shaping my understanding of right from wrong. With Mum and Dad experiencing significant health issues, I became a carer at a young age, setting up a family scenario that few, if any, of my friends understood.

Your family context will have been different from mine, but I am sure you can reflect on how your family dynamic has directly or indirectly impacted your identity. Your family experience may be positive or negative, but what remains true will be that our experience of family is the first identity shaper that each of us encounters.

## Identity Shaper 2: Demographics
**Our demographic background shapes our understanding of who we are.**

The Cambridge Dictionary defines demographics as:

*'The number and characteristics of people who live in a particular area or form a particular group, especially in relation to their age, how much money they have and what they spend it on.'* [1]

Whether you grew up, like me, in a rural village or a large multi-cultural city, it has a direct impact on your identity. If you had many siblings or none, it directly impacts who you are today. Whether you grew up in a one-bedroom flat or a mansion, it affects your identity today. Growing up in abject poverty or with overflowing riches will also directly impact who you are today.

Regardless of the demographic indicator we choose to look at[2] — and there are many — the measurement of that indicator in relation to your past and present position has an impact on shaping who you are.

---

[1] https://dictionary.cambridge.org/dictionary/english/demographics

[2] Some examples of demographic indicators include age, race, ethnicity, gender, marital status, income, education, and employment.

## Identity Shaper 3: Social Status
**Our social status shapes the lens through which we see life.**

How we see ourselves in relation to others within society has a direct impact on our identity.

Sociologists suggest there are five social classes: upper class, upper-middle-class, lower-middle-class, working-class and poor.

Over the trajectory of our lives, it is possible to transcend classes; but it is likely the societal class we grew up in will have had a significant impact on our identity. Many people are fiercely proud of their class roots and want to be identified by their original social class even though they may have moved up a class because of education or employment.

**Community:** I believe the three communities of people that shape our identity most are our friends, our educators and the of faith we belong to. Each of these communities has and will continue to play key roles in our understanding of who we are and the shaping of who we become.

## Identity Shaper 4: Friends
**The friends we choose will shape who we are and who we become.**

As a child, I had some good friends, but not a large circle of them. My closest childhood friend shaped my identity because I followed him in supporting Leeds United. That has been a journey of ups and mainly downs over the last 50 years, I can tell you!

As you reflect throughout your life, I wonder how your choice of friends has shaped who you are? Some friends will have had a positive impact on your life, while others may well have had a negative one on who you have become. Each friend, in some way, will have played their part in shaping your identity.

## Identity Shaper 5: Education
**Educators not only teach students, they shape the lives of students.**

Our experience of education, and teachers, has, I believe, a profound impact on the shaping of our identity. Your first teachers, in school or Sunday school, are likely to have played a role in shaping your perception of education, and, as a result, the extent to which you engaged positively or not with education. Even now, I am sure you remember the faces and names of teachers who you recall from childhood who shaped your opinion of teachers. As a result, they shaped your engagement with it.

As we progressed through our childhood and teenage years into adulthood, the impact – positive or negative – of education will have continued to shape our identity. It will either have given us more confidence or caused us to lack confidence.

## Identity Shaper 6: Faith
**Our experience of faith will shape the faith with which we lead.**

Some of us will have grown up in homes where faith was central to everything. For others, faith was peripheral to life, while some people have grown up in homes where faith was not a discussion. As children, we may have encountered people of faith who were 'saint like'; others may, sadly, have experienced people of faith who abused their power and authority. For many, faith will have been a religious experience, but for some, it will have been a lived experience of relationship with God through His son Jesus

Regardless of our experience of faith to this point, it is true to say that faith, or its absence, has shaped our identity, and will continue to mould and shape our identity throughout our lives.

**Culture:** The word culture is used in many contexts. But for the purpose of considering what has shaped our identity, we consider culture to be 'the social behaviour and norms found in human societies, as well as the knowledge, beliefs, arts, laws, customs, capabilities, and habits of the individuals in these groups.'

## Identity Shaper 7: Influences
**The influences around us shape the identity within us.**

I grew up in a community that prided itself on its culture. Although citizens of Northern Ireland (formerly part of the Irish province of Ulster), most of the people who lived in my area were of Scottish extraction and known as 'Ulster Scots'. They were characterised by loyalty to the Queen and to the customs they saw as being part of a culture under attack from those seeking to reunite Ireland. Unsurprisingly, growing up in such an environment, I became committed and dedicated to participating in and defending the culture. For many years, my identity was closely aligned with my culture.

As you look back over your youth, there may well have been one or more cultural expressions that shaped your early life. Perhaps it continues to shape your life today.

## Identity Shaper 8: Traditions
**Our traditions either empower our future or trap us in our past.**

In every family, community and nation, there are traditions. Many of these are good traditions, although some may have been better consigned to history. The merit, or not, of the traditions that have shaped our lives is of less importance than the impact these traditions have on shaping our identity and, as a result, the journey of our lives.

If the tradition we hold on to equips and empowers our future, then that is a tradition to be celebrated. If, however, the tradition we hold onto traps us in loyalty to the past or to forces that are not for our good, then that is a tradition best laid down.

## Identity Shaper 9: Expectations
**Cultures where expectancy is low tend to develop people with low expectancy.**

Our level of expectation is, in part, determined by our past experiences and the cultural influences that we have encountered. Some will have grown up in a culture where little was expected and, often, little accomplished. Others will have grown up in a culture where a lot was expected of them, sometimes leading to much being achieved, which, sadly, placed too heavy a burden of expectation on them.

The level of expectancy we have will continue to shape our identity. As we consider later, our level of expectancy is something we need to continue to monitor, lest we become those who fear failure more than we embrace the future with expectancy.

**Choices:** Leadership speaker and author, John C Maxwell, once said, "Life is a matter of choices, and every choice you make makes you."

For all of us, I believe this is true. We are, to some extent, the product of our choices. Every day we make choices that have an impact upon our lives. Some of these impacts could be regarded as minor or trivial: for example, whether we eat pasta or rice with a meal. Other choices have a much greater significance: who you choose to marry, for example.

As we look at the final three 'Identity Shapers', I believe each of them is related to choices: the choices made for us, the choices that impact on us and the choices we make.

## Identity Shaper 10: Choices Made for You
Choices made for you, by parents, educators or employers.

When we were children, most of the choices that affected us were made by our parents. Choices about how they parented us, what they fed us, and how we dressed. As we grew older and went to school, another group of people became involved in making choices for us. How we spent our time, the classes we went to and choice of teachers was made for us until such times as we were considered old enough to decide for ourselves. Moving on from full-time education, we entered employment. Bosses then made decisions for us, such as the hours we worked, the nature of the work and the level of income we received for our employment.

At every stage of life, choices are being made for us that shape our lives and ultimately shape our identity.

## Identity Shaper 11: Choices That Impact You
**Choices that impact on you, for example those made by people groups and government.**

Beyond our immediate circle of influence, decision-makers make choices that impact us that we have little or no influence over. These, too, shape our identity. As an example, 100 years ago, a decision was taken to divide the island of Ireland. This decision was not one that my forefathers had any direct control over, but it is a decision that impacted each person who lives in the two parts of the island ever since. Events like this can shape not only our identity but the perception that others have of our identity.

In other parts of the world, nations have chosen to ban the expression of the Christian faith. This decision has had a direct impact on the identity of millions over many decades. Yet it was not an identity change they had any control over.

## Identity Shaper 12: Choices Made by You
**Choice made by you as a result of your context, community or culture.**

Finally, in our consideration of identity shapers, we come to the role that the choices we make have in shaping our identity. All of us live in a world shaped by our context, our community and our culture. Consequently, when we make choices, they will likely be influenced, to some extent, by the context, community or culture shapers that we have experienced. As no one will have experienced the same set of circumstances concerning context, community and culture, the sum of all of our choices will lead each of us to have a unique identity.

It is said that every decision we make has the power to impact our identity positively or negatively.

## ...And finally

Before considering how an encounter with Jesus can change our identity, I would invite you to take time to consider how each of the 12 Identity Shapers, listed below, has impacted your life.

|  | Impact on Your Identity | | |
|---|---|---|---|
| **Identity Shaper** | **Significant** | **Some** | **Little** |
| 1. Family | | | |
| 2. Demographics | | | |
| 3. Social Status | | | |
| 4. Friends | | | |
| 5. Education | | | |
| 6. Faith | | | |
| 7. Influences | | | |
| 8. Traditions | | | |
| 9. Expectations | | | |
| 10. Choices made for you | | | |
| 11. Choices that impact you | | | |
| 12. Choices made by you | | | |

*If you have received Jesus as your Lord and Saviour, your identity has now been transformed.*

## Chapter 2
# Identity Transformed

Your context, community, culture and choices may have had a significant role in shaping your identity. But if you have received Jesus as your Lord and Saviour, your identity has now been transformed.

Who you were is being continually transformed into the likeness of Jesus. If your name is Mary Brown, you are known to people as Mary Brown – but you are, in fact, Mary Brown, a daughter of the King of Kings and a co-heir with Christ!

Understanding the 'identity transformation' that takes place through salvation can release us from many of the negative experiences that have shaped our identity and release us into the freedom that is found in Christ alone.

It has been my experience that the more I embrace my identity in Christ, the more I can live and lead like Jesus. At various times over the last 50 years of trusting Jesus, I have leaned back towards aspects of my identity formation, rather than the identity transformation that occurred when I received Jesus as my Saviour. When I think back to my teenage years, I identified myself, at times, with the culture of my forefathers rather than with the culture of the kingdom of heaven. As a result, this led me to the edge of involvement in things that could be considered illegal. I am eternally grateful to God for the Holy Spirit calling me back to my true identity in Christ.

In this chapter, we will consider 9 wonderful truths about who we have become through Jesus Christ.

## 1. Through Jesus, we are set free

Before you met Jesus, you were trapped by the snare of the enemy and by your selfish ambitions, but in Jesus, we have been set free. If you choose to live life without the knowledge of your identity in Christ, you will find yourself repeatedly being led back towards sin and selfishness. If you live your life in the identity you have through Jesus Christ, you will live life that is pleasing to God and that serves His Kingdom purposes rather than your own.

As a 'Jesus-centred leader', you need to continue to live in the freedom for which Christ has set you free, so that you might bring glory to Him and you might live and lead through His grace and wisdom.

In John 3:38, Jesus said, "So if the Son sets you free, you will be free indeed."

To this, I say, "Hallelujah!"

## 2. Through Jesus, we are set apart.

Back in my primary school playground, I remember being 'set apart' but not in a good way. You see, as the least athletic of the boys in my class, I was always 'set apart'. In other words, I was even left until last when pupils were being chosen for football. Sometimes I wasn't even picked and was left to stand apart from everyone else. Then as I entered post-primary school, I remember me and a few friends being 'set apart', again in a negative sense, by a group of bullies. Each day, at lunchtime, they locked us in a storage room under the rugby pavilion.

However, in Jesus, you are set apart not for a negative reason, for the glory of God. In doing so, God has transformed your identity from a person who had no future and no hope to being a person who has within you the hope of glory. When you begin to grasp this reality, it enables you to set aside all the negative experiences of your past lives and focus on the greater things yet to come.

As 'Jesus-centred leaders', you need to realise that not only have you been set apart but why you have been set apart. In 1 Peter 2:9, it says that we are 'a chosen race, a royal priesthood, a holy nation, a people for His possession.'

The next time the enemy tries to tell you that you are not qualified to lead, remind him that, through Jesus, you are a paid-up full member of a chosen race: part a royal priesthood, a holy nation and His possession.

## 3. Through Jesus, we are sent out.

In 1986, I took a summer job working at a local petrol garage. Each morning, at around 10 am, we would have a tea break – coffee wasn't that popular in Northern Ireland back then. My colleague, Billy, was renowned for enjoying his tea, a bun or two and a laugh. Inevitably, the 15-minute tea break never ended in 15 minutes unless the boss was around. If Jimmy, the boss, appeared, he would have been quick to remind us that he 'wasn't paying us to sit about'.

In Jesus, you are designed to be sent out to fulfil the purposes of God. Not only has God chosen you and set you apart, but he has also entrusted you with His

Kingdom business. Too often, you get comfortable in your new identity in Christ but fail to embrace the 'send out' part.

If you have come this far in this book, however, I believe that you have embraced the 'sent' part of your identity, as described by Jesus in John 17:18

'As you sent me into the world, so I have sent them.'

As a result of identity transformation' you can be assured that God has a plan and purpose for you and that he will enable you to see His Kingdom come on earth as it is in heaven.

## 4. As sons and daughters, we are loved.

Some of you who are reading this book will have different experiences of the love of earthly parents. For some, that love will have been a wonderful thing: whether expressed through a natural father, mother, or both; through the love of a paternal or maternal relative; or the love of a foster/adoptive family. Some of you will not have had such a positive experience of being loved as a son or daughter. Others may have experienced, like me, the pain of losing parents early in life.

In Jesus, however, you encounter the perfect love of the heavenly Father. A love that will never diminish and the love of a lover who will never seek to use us or abuse us. Through the love of the Father, we can know healing and wholeness from the pain and loss of the love we have experienced naturally.

As you seek to live and lead like Jesus, it is worthwhile taking time on a regular basis to dwell on the depth of some of the most famous words of Jesus, as recorded in John 3:16...

*'For God so loved the world.'*

Thank you, Lord!

## 5. As sons and daughters, we are chosen.

The word 'chosen' brings to mind the thought that the person has been 'chosen', whereas others have not. If this were a theological text, we would take time to look at theological views on such weighty matters as predestination and eternal security. But the thrust of this book is one in which you can be encouraged, equipped and empowered to live and lead more like Jesus.

I believe we can all draw great encouragement from the words of Jesus in John 15:16, when he said, "You did not choose me, but I chose you."

This raises our gratitude to God in that he has chosen each of us, as His sons and daughters, to live and lead like Jesus. As the Miriam-Webster dictionary says, we are 'one who is the object of choice or of divine favour'. What wonderful news! God's divine favour rests upon us. Our identity transformation has caused us to be those that God chooses to bestow His favour.

The Collins dictionary says that those who are chosen are 'selected or picked out, for some special quality'. Within each of us, God has chosen to place gifts and talents that, when surrendered to him, will bring glory to the name of Jesus.

## 6. As sons and daughters, we are family.

I was an only child. Growing up, I did not think much of that. I did not feel any different from my friends who had brothers and sisters. But my identity was undoubtedly shaped by being in a family where I was the only offspring. I had no way of knowing what it would be like to have a brother or sister, other than my second-hand experience of regularly staying with a childhood friend who had an older and younger sister. Honestly, I reckoned it was better to be an only child!

Whatever your family context, your identity has been transformed as a son and daughter of God into those who are a part of the family of God. As we grow in relationship with God and others, he helps you understand the dynamics of the heavenly family that you now belong to: one in which we are all equally loved and equally valued.

What a joy it is to read in Ephesians 1:5 that we have experienced, "Adoption as sons through Jesus Christ."


You and I are brothers and sisters, not because of anything we have done, but because of what Jesus has done for us. Together, as a family, you can see the transformational power of Jesus at work in your home, workplace, community and church.

## 7. As joint heirs, we are seated in heavenly places.

Has anyone ever told you to go, sit down and be quiet? These are words I remember well from many years ago; words that were spoken frivolously by a leader who probably thought nothing more of what they had said. Yet words like these have been used countless times over the years to cause people like you and me to think that we had nothing to say. They caused us to remain seated when God has called us to stand up and declare the words of wisdom he has placed within us.

Words like these may have caused you to feel that you are not adequate, not good enough or smart enough. Words like these may have trapped you in insecurity and robbed you of becoming who you are truly called to be. No more!

Today, I believe God would have you see yourself as a joint heir with Jesus, seated in heavenly places with Him. Your inheritance in Christ does not take effect when you get to heaven. It took effect when you accept Jesus, God's gift of grace. You are already a joint-heir. It is time to see yourself seated in a heavenly place, not shrinking at the back of the room but taking your places among those who God has raised in these days to live and lead like Jesus.

Ephesians 2:6 reminds us, "God raised us up with Christ and seated us with him in the heavenly realms in Christ Jesus."

Rather than seeing yourself as inferior, it is time to see yourself as a son or daughter of All Mighty God, seated in heavenly places. Now is your time to arise!

## 8. As joint heirs, we rule and reign with Christ.

Your identity has been transformed through Christ for a purpose. Sadly, many believe that salvation is nothing more than a one-way ticket to heaven. *It is so much more than that!* God has transformed your identity for a purpose. When you fully embrace the purpose for your identity as being transformed, you can begin to truly live out the potential of your new identity in Christ.

Over the last 20 years, I have had the opportunity to teach in many Bible schools and church-based leadership programmes. Regardless of where I have travelled globally, I have found that the churches and colleges I have taught in have a strong legacy of sound biblical and theological teaching on the grace of God and righteousness. Students have been well-grounded in understanding that in God, they live and minister through God's grace as those who have been made righteous through the imputed righteousness of Jesus. However, in Romans 5:17, we read about the purpose of grace and righteousness, "Those who receive God's abundant provision of grace and the gift of righteousness reign in life through the one man, Jesus Christ."

You are equipped and empowered by God, in your transformed identity, to rule and reign in life through Jesus Christ. Your life and your leadership, centred on Jesus, means that you can walk in victory even during trials and tribulation because your victory is not found in circumstances, but through the revelation that you rule and reign with Christ.

Now, that's good news!

## 9. As joint heirs, we operate through God's authority.

"Who said you could?" This is a question that can immediately put you on the back foot unless you have been given authority by a person in power. Without that authority, you would have no right to do what you are doing.

So, too, it is for those of us who are the sons and daughters of God. You have no authority in your own right, but you have been given power and authority by God, through Jesus. Your identity has been transformed from people without authority to those with authority. The very authority that Jesus had on this earth has been given to you as a co-heir with Him.

In the natural, there are many things that you may not feel equipped to do. There may have been, and there certainly will be, times when you do not think you have the ability to do what you are asked to do. However, the Bible tells us that 'greater things than these shall you do'. Why? Because we have been empowered by God himself to walk by faith and see the impossible come to pass.

Mark 16:15-18 sets out the authority that we have been given, "He said to them, 'Go into all the world and preach the gospel to all creation. Whoever believes and is baptised will be saved, but whoever does not believe will be condemned. And these signs will accompany those who believe: In my name they will drive out demons; they will speak in new tongues; they will pick up snakes with their hands; and when they drink deadly poison, it will not hurt them at all; they will place their hands-on sick people, and they will get well.'"

As you conclude this chapter on identity transformation, know that as a son or daughter of God you have been given the authority and power to do all that God would have you do. So, no longer allow the enemy to make you feel weak and inadequate.

*God wants, through the wisdom he has made available ... to release witty inventions that will result in His children bringing solutions to every area of life.*

## Chapter 3
# Identity Empowered

I grew up in a world influenced by TV and the programmes being produced in the 1970s and 80s. Quite a number of these programmes featured what we now refer to as 'superheroes'. Whether it was Batman, Spiderman, Superman or any other, each took on a new identity – just as we have taken on a new identity in Christ.

Each superhero also received superhero abilities and powers, however, that set them apart from everyone else. As a son and daughter of God, you have been given supernatural abilities and powers that set you apart from the world around you. Your identity, as a son or daughter, is being continually empowered by God through His wisdom, His favour, the Holy Spirit and the gifts that God releases into your life. When you embrace the supernatural abilities and power that God has given you, you can live and lead with greater confidence, bringing glory to God in all that you do.

In this chapter, we will consider the abilities and power that God has imparted to those of us who have surrendered our lives to Jesus and know, with even greater assurance, that God has empowered us to live and lead with the confidence that can only come from an identity rooted in Jesus.

## Our identity has been empowered by God's wisdom

- **God's wisdom is available to His sons and daughters**

You may have heard people remark how a child has their mother's looks father's brains or vice versa. The truth, however, that a child's looks and intelligence are derived from both their father and mother.

There are many things you have inherited from your parents: some good and some not so good! What you can be assured of, however, is that everything you have been given by our heavenly Father is good. One such good gift is God's wisdom.

We read about Solomon in the Bible: a King living under the old Covenant, seeking and receiving God's wisdom, causing Him to be regarded as the wisest man in the world. To even consider that the creator of the universe would give His wisdom to a man is incredible. What is more incredible is the reality that under the new Covenant, God's wisdom is freely available to anyone who lacks wisdom!

In James 1:5 we are told that: *"If any of you lacks wisdom, you should ask God, who gives generously to all without finding fault, and it will be given to you."*

Three things stand out for me in this verse:

(i) Anyone can ask God for wisdom.

(ii) God will give His wisdom generously.

(iii) God will give His wisdom without finding fault in us.

I would encourage you each day to ask God for wisdom, knowing that he will give it generously and give it without finding fault in you. What a God we serve!

- **God's wisdom gives us the advantage (not available to others)**

I was recently watching an international rugby match between Wales and Ireland. Early in the game, Ireland was reduced to 14 players. This gave Wales an advantage. Despite Ireland coming back to lead at half-time, the Welsh side had the advantage of an extra man, meaning they eventually came out as winners.

Having an extra man on your side is advantageous, but what if that extra man is God himself? That may seem too much to believe, but that is the wonderful supernatural reality of where we find ourselves as sons and daughters of God.

You are not alone! God is with you wherever you go. His wisdom rests upon you and is available to you. When you are in a difficult situation His wisdom is available to you and will guide and instruct you in what you should say or do. His wisdom will cause you to excel when other cannot.

In life, we all experience many difficulties, but as a son and daughter of God, you have an advantage that the world does not have because God's wisdom has been reserved for God's children.

- **God's wisdom releases witty inventions**

That is a great idea! I have a friend called Matt. He is one of those people who seems to come up with great ideas overnight that are simple but profound. These ideas can help improve life for thousands of people. People like that are often few and far between, a rare commodity.

'Ideas people' are needed by every organisation. Fresh ideas can give you and the organisation you lead a competitive advantage or can help you solve issues that no one else has ever been able to solve.

In the book of Proverbs, we read about 'bright ideas' or as chapter 8 verse 12 calls them witty inventions: "I, wisdom, dwell with prudence, and find out knowledge of witty inventions."

In history, we find many of the greatest inventors were Christians. Was this by chance? No! I believe it was because they received witty inventions from God, which enabled them to become world-renowned inventors. Many of their inventions changed the course of history.

I believe that God wants, through the wisdom he has made available to those who love and trust Him, to release witty inventions that will result in His children bringing solutions to every area of life. Join me in asking God to release to you witty inventions that will change the world!

## Our identity has been empowered by God's favour

- God's favour rests upon you

The dictionary defines favour as approval, support, or liking for someone or something. It also suggests favour is an act of kindness beyond what is due or usual.

Wow! That sounds good to me. <u>Far and above the favour of man is the favour that we receive from God!</u>

God's favour — or God's favur if you live in North America — is a concept that many Christians find hard to understand and embrace. However, scripture shows me that God's favour rests upon us, not momentarily, but throughout our lives.

Psalm 30 verse 5 says, "For His anger is but for a moment, and His favour is for a lifetime."

What a remarkable contrast! God's anger is momentary, but God's favour lasts throughout our lifetime. When you place your life in God's hands, making Him our Saviour, His anger passes as you are no longer a sinner. But you have been transformed into sons and daughters of the King of Kings. Yes, you may still sin, but your nature has been transformed, and God's anger has passed. In its place, he releases His favour on you, which rests upon you for the rest of your life.

When the enemy tries to bring guilt and shame upon you, remind Him of who you are. Do not be bowed down under the weight of condemnation that the enemy wants to bring. Instead, rise up in the knowledge that God's favour rests upon you and God's favour goes before you.

- **God's favour will bring you before great men**

They are well connected! Now there is a phrase you may hear about someone successful in a particular area of life.

If you had known me as an only child growing up in rural Northern Ireland during a civil conflict with two sick parents, you would not have said I was well connected – I was completely unconnected. I had no family, business or social connections that could help me 'make it' in life.

Perhaps you were like me. But now as a son and daughter of God, you are connected through relationship to Him and millions of brothers and sisters around the world. The greatest relational network you can ever be part of is the family of God.

In my life and leadership journey over the past 30-plus years, I have seen God open up doors of opportunity where His favour caused me to meet people and do things I could never have imagined. When he opens the door, it's not a struggle – it is a joy!

I genuinely believe that God wants to take you places that you never imagined. Without a doubt, I know that that is God's plan for your life. How do I know? Proverbs 22:29 tells me, "Do you see a man skilful in his work? He will stand before kings; he will not stand before obscure men."

When you and I work with wisdom and excellence, the favour that God has placed upon our lives will cause us to stand before great men (and women). Think of Joseph: raised from obscurity to rule over Egypt; think of Moses: raised from certain death to lead the people of Israel out of captivity. When we surrender ourselves to God, there is no telling where he can take us or where he can lead us.

- **God's favour will cause you to succeed when others fail**

When I was training in pastoral ministry back in the late 1980s, I would occasionally be allowed to preach in small churches of the denomination of which I was a member. An older friend, who was also training in pastoral ministry, seemed to get more opportunities to speak than me. When I asked him about it, he said that 'if the door didn't open, he kicked it down.'

Like my friend, you can take things into your own hands and try to force doors to open, or you can choose to trust God to open doors. Whilst the forceful approach may seem to be more advantageous in the short term, I believe that trusting God will cause you to be more successful long term. In my lifetime, I have witnessed many Christians who tried to succeed through their own efforts. It may seem to have worked for a period but, ultimately, it brought that person to a place of pain and despair.

Whatever area of life you are engaged in, I believe that God's favour is the best door opener you can ever experience. He can cause you to succeed in your family, your life, business and your ministry if you trust in His leading and favour.

## Our identity has been empowered by the Holy Spirit

### • The Holy Spirit is our counsellor, teacher and guide

There are many things you witness in nature that you do not understand. I recently watched a documentary about a species of fish that has appeared, as if from nowhere, in large numbers in the Caribbean. The fish has poisonous fins, but when they are removed and it is cooked, it provides a very nutritious meal. Somehow, God, in His wisdom, decided to create that species of fish in that unique way.

So, too, each of us has been created as unique. Not one of us is the same, but God has chosen to place within each of us the gift of the Holy Spirit. My mind cannot fathom how that is possible, but I know that it is. My heart has a calm reassurance that God has chosen, despite all our failings, to place within us the Holy Spirit, who empowers our identity with the power of heaven. Whatever situation we are facing right now, we can know, with assurance, that the Holy Spirit is working in and through us. He is our counsellor, our teacher and our guide. There is nothing we cannot face when he is with us.

John 14:16-17 says, "I will ask the Father, and he will give you another Helper, that he may be with you forever; that is the Spirit of truth, whom the world cannot receive, because it does not see Him or know Him, but you know Him because he abides with you and will be in you."

What a joy it is to know that the Holy Spirit abides in us, will be with us and that he is assigned by the Father to be our helper!

## • The Holy Spirit is our advocate

An advocate is a word that we do not use in everyday language. If you are familiar with the legal system, you may have encountered it when lawyers, solicitors or barristers are mentioned.

The Merriam Webster dictionary defines the word in three ways[3]:

→ One who pleads the cause of another

→ One who defends or maintains a cause or proposal

→ One who supports or promotes the interests of a cause or group

When you consider this in light of who you are through Jesus Christ, it helps you understand that God has sent the Holy Spirit to plead your cause, defend you and support you. Not only have you been adopted into the family of God, but He has sent His Holy Spirit to champion you!

For years, people may have put you down. The enemy may have beaten you further down through attacks on your mind, your will and your emotions. But as you read this, know that God, through the Holy Spirit, is raising you up so that you can stand in the fullness of His power, knowing that he is championing you!

John 14: 26 says, "But the Advocate, the Holy Spirit, whom the Father will send in my name, will teach you all things and will remind you of everything I have said to you."

---

[3] https://www.merriam-webster.com/dictionary/advocate

What a promise! The Holy Spirit is our advocate and He will teach you all things! That is that truth that each of us can walk in when we know our identity has been transformed and empowered by God.

- **The Holy Spirit is our unique source of power**

Early in this chapter, I referred to superheroes! What made them super was that they had power that no one else had. That made them stand out from everyone else and made them able to do things that no one else could.

I passionately believe that God has designed you and me to stand out from the crowd. He has given you powers that no one else has. He has given you unique gifts, which, when released through the power of the Holy Spirit, allows you to do things others cannot.

I believe that God is calling His Church to awake to the power that he has given them. These are days when I think believers will see the supernatural power of God at work in their families, workplaces, communities and churches. I believe these are the days when we, the Church, will walk in the 'greater things than these' that Jesus referred to before he ascended to heaven.

Now is your time to awaken to your transformed and empowered identity, for greater things are yet to come!

## Our identity has been empowered by God's gifts

Finally, in this chapter, we want to give thanks to God for the gifts he gives us. He truly is a good Father. Ephesians

4:8 tells us that, "When he ascended on high, he took many captives and gave gifts to His people."

God did not leave you without the gifts that you need. He intentionally gave you gifts so you could live and lead like Jesus. Each gift comes quality assured by God. James 1:17 explains, "Every good gift and every perfect gift is from above."

In addition to the nine gifts of the Holy Spirit listed in 1 Corinthians 11, the Bible also lists a range of gifts that God gives to His children including:

- Administration / Ruling
- Apostleship / Pioneering
- Discernment
- Encouraging / Exhorting
- Evangelism
- Faith
- Giving
- Hospitality
- Knowledge
- Leadership
- Pastor / Shepherding
- Prophecy / Perceiving
- Teaching
- Serving / Ministry
- Showing Mercy
- Wisdom

Each of us has different gifts, according to the grace God has given to us (Romans 12:6). But each we can live and lead like Jesus, knowing that God's gifts set us apart from others. His gifts enable you to do what others cannot, and they help you hear, see and do things that are impossible for others.

# Section 2 : Inspiration

*A true leader is not necessarily someone who accomplishes great things, but someone who inspires others to accomplish great things.*

# Chapter 4
# Being Inspired

## Inspired to be who you are

When you were growing up, who inspired you? It is said that those who inspire us in early life set the course for our life. It may have been the case for you. Someone who inspired you as a child or young person may have put you on a course to the career, hobby or passion that has become central to your life. You may know someone who was inspired at school by a teacher. They may have inspired them to become a teacher or follow a career in the subject that the teacher taught.

As a boy growing up in the 1970s, I was inspired by several people who helped shape my life. One was a Methodist minister who became the minister in my home church in 1977.

Ken had just returned from missionary work in the West Indies, where he lived with his wife and young children. He was very different from any minister I had known before. His compassionate pastoral style, along with his clear easy to understand teaching, grabbed my attention through my early post-primary school years. Much of how I lead and teach today has roots in the style that inspired me all those years ago.

When it came to football, I was inspired by my friend Alister to support Leeds United! At the time, they were one of the best football clubs in England. I was inspired to dedicate time to supporting the club. This support has lasted 50 years, even though during the last 16 years,

Leeds have struggled to return to Premier League football.

## Inspired from on high

As someone seeking to live and lead like Jesus, your greatest source of inspiration comes from your relationship with Him as well as your revelation of who you are in Him. In Sunday school, Bible stories were an inspiration, but as I grew to know God personally, I began to be inspired by the life of Jesus. Knowing how I could live and lead through Jesus then became my inspiration.

In the book of Job, a book not read by many, we read in Chapter 32:8, "But there is a spirit in man: and the inspiration of the Almighty giveth them understanding."

What a glorious thought: to know that the Spirit of God lives within you and that you can receive divine inspiration from the Almighty himself! As you walk and talk with God daily, you are inspired by Him through the power of the Holy Spirit. Your inspiration is not drawn from or focused on the inspiration you have received from others, good as that may be. Your inspiration, instead, is drawn from and focused on God. This is what sets you apart from those who are not sons and daughters of God. You have the advantage of being inspired by the creator of the universe. As a believer, you have the creative genius of the Master creator inspiring you. You have the ability and capacity to be a leading creative mind on earth today. From God, you can receive inspiration to solve problems others cannot solve and to create things others cannot create.

Being inspired from on high is such an honour and a privilege, yet God chooses to do so. Why? Because he loves you unconditionally as His child! Just as a parent wants the best for their child, the Heavenly Father wants the absolute best for you. He wants you to be inspired so that you can bring transformational change to lives, communities, cities and nations. And he wants you to be inspired so that you can see His Kingdom come on earth as it is in heaven.

Each day we are further inspired by the Spirit of God as we read the Bible. 2 Timothy 3:16 tells us, "All scripture is given by inspiration of God, and is profitable for doctrine, for reproof, for correction, for instruction in righteousness."

Being inspired from on high comes through your daily walk with God and your study of His inspired Word. God's Word inspires you to live a pattern of life that inspires you so that you can encourage others. The blessing of living through God's Word means you have been made righteous through Jesus.

When the enemy seeks to sow words of doubt and discouragement in your spirit, you need to remind him that you are a son and daughter of God. Indeed, you are inspired by Him to live and lead in this life! The time has come to be encouraged by the truth that your inspiration comes from on high, and you are destined to a person of divine inspiration who can be a world changer.

## Being Inspired is Essential

It is rare for people to be inspired by uninspiring people, so being inspired is essential to influence others.

Steve Maraboli, a US military veteran, behaviour scientist and speaker says, "When you are living the best version of yourself, you inspire others to live the best versions of themselves."

When you are being inspired each day by God and taking steps to be influenced by others, I believe you can be the best version of yourself. As a result, you can inspire others to accomplish great things. A true leader is not necessarily someone who accomplishes great things, but someone who inspires others to accomplish great things.

The dictionary refers to inspiration as 'the process of being mentally stimulated to do or feel something, especially to do something creative'.[4] For the children of God, however, I believe inspiration is more than a mental process. Inspiration comes from the Spirit of God within you; it is derived from a much deeper well than the inspiration others derive through mental stimulation.

To be inspired each day it is important to remember that:

- Inspiration is divine
- Inspiration is essential
- Inspiration is fuel for life

I believe that those of us inspired by God achieve more than those who are inspired by other sources of lesser

---

[4] Oxford English Dictionary

inspiration. Nothing in this world, including the offerings of other religions and meditative practices, can compare to the inspiration you have received and will continue to receive from your Heavenly Father.

Being God-inspired:

- Is a blessing of living a life surrender to God;
- Will lead you to have success when others do not have success;
- Leads you to create what no one else could create;
- Will lead you to be promoted when others are not promoted;
- Leads to doors opening for you that won't open for others.

That is a life I want to live, and it is a life each you can live as you remain Jesus-centred in all you seek to do.

## Being Inspired: My Own Journey

People often ask me how I have continued, over many years, to speak, write and post words each day that encourage and inspire others. The answer is simple: I seek to be inspired daily by Jesus and others who live and lead like Jesus.

I have intentionally chosen to be encouraged each day by Jesus-centred inspiration. It is a choice that requires dedication, focus and making an ongoing decision to close out voices that are discouraging, negative and uninspiring. The Bible says that we should 'renew our minds' and so I have had to purpose in my heart to allow my mind to be renewed by Jesus-centred inspiration.

I have done this by:

- Being inspired by the life of Jesus
- Being inspired by the love of Jesus
- Being inspired by the words of Jesus
- Being inspired by the life of Christian brothers and sisters
- Being inspired by the love of Christian brothers and sisters
- Being inspired by the words of Christian brothers and sisters

Jesus-centred inspiration is an essential input to the life of those who seek to live and lead like Him. Carefully choose what you allow your ears to hear and your eyes to see. You will then live the best life that God intended for you, and you can lead others to live the best life God intended for them.

## The True Purpose of Being Inspired

Depending on what tradition you grew up in, you may have learned the Westminster Shorter Catechism. In the Catechism, the question is asked, "What is the chief end of man?" The answer given is, "Man's chief end is to glorify God, and to enjoy him forever."

In life, you aspire to glorify God in all we do. But this is not something God expects you to do without His help. I believe He inspires you so you can glorify Him. It could be said that being inspired by God has its true purpose in glorifying God.

I believe that you are being inspired by God to:

## 1. To live a life that honours and respects God

As those who love God, I can think of no better reason for being inspired by Him than to bring honour to God. He is worthy of all the honour! To give Him honour should be your heart's desire, even if there is no reward for doing so. In 1 Samuel, however, we read that God says that 'he who honours Him, he will he honour'. Not only will he honour you, but He has established an everlasting covenant with you. You can be assured that as you continue to honour Him, He will continue to honour you. In Jeremiah 32:40 we read, "I will make an everlasting covenant with them: I will never stop doing good to them, and I will inspire them to fear me, so that they will never turn away from me."

What a God we serve! He inspires you to fear Him. Fear, as used in Jeremiah, is based on the Hebrew for 'honour and respect'. What a joy to know that God inspires you so that you can honour and respect Him, and when you do, he will never stop doing good to you!

## 2. To live a life inspired by God's wisdom

I am not sure about you, but I was never an A-grade student — more a C-grader!

However, I am thankful that, in Jesus, we can draw upon the inspiration that God gives and allows His wisdom to flow through you. In these last days, I believe that God is calling you to be inspired by Him so that you can display His wisdom, not for our glory, but for His honour and glory.

### 3. To live a life that inspires others

There are few greater joys than to inspire others to be all that God has empowered them to be. Being inspired by God has helped me to do just that. I believe that as you seek to continue to be inspired by Jesus and Jesus-centred brothers and sisters, you will see a generation rise up.

### 4. To live a life that release God's kingdom on earth as it is in heaven

In the prayer that Jesus taught His disciples, we pray 'thy kingdom come on earth as it is in heaven'. Having been inspired by God, let us be those who seek to see God's kingdom come on earth as it is heaven. <u>The time for churches to build religious monuments and silos is over. The time for the Church to unite to see God's kingdom come is now.</u>

### 5. To live a life that sees the Church at work every day, everywhere

Back in 2013, I was contacted via Twitter by someone from Australia who was unknown to me. As it happened, David McCracken was born in Northern Ireland but has lived much of his life in New Zealand and Australia. He has become a great friend, mentor and prophetic voice in my life.

David has been a conference speaker and passionate voice for the Kingdom of God for many years. He loves the Church but sees it as being so much more than a Sunday gathering. Recently he said, "Sunday is not 'The

Church'. Sunday inspires and equips the Church to Be 'The Church' on Monday!"

Like David, I believe that we are being inspired by God, as the Church, so that we can be the Church every day of the week. That can be for your family, community or workplace. To limit the inspiration of God to a Sunday limits the power of God. Let us be inspired by God to be His Church wherever we go.

### 6. To live a life that endures, through inspiration

In the business world, much thought has been given to the subject of resilience. Indeed, countless books have been published and conferences held about it. Resilience is the capacity to recover quickly from difficulties. In the sporting world, many words have been written and said about endurance, which means to have the ability to endure an unpleasant or difficult process or situation without giving way.

Being inspired, according to 1 Thessalonians 1:3, gives you 'hope that leads to endurance'. How amazing to think that not only can you recover quickly from difficulties, but you have the ability to endure unpleasant and difficult processes and situations. Through inspiration by God you can stand the test of time.

When the writer to the Hebrews says, 'let us therefore run the race set before us,' you have the assurance that being inspired by God gives you the resilience and endurance to do so.

## 7. To live a life that speaks words that foretell God's plans

To be inspired by God gives you the ability to speak prophetically into the lives of others. Revelation 22:6 talks about 'God who inspires the prophets'. With God's inspiration, you can call out God's best for the lives of those you meet and those you lead. Through divine inspiration, you can see what God sees in people. Speaking that forward, you can see people released from the captivity of their past and released into their divine destiny.

## Prayer

*Father, we are so blessed to know that not only do you love us, but you continually inspire us. We thank you for the inspiration we receive through the Holy Spirit and through the life, love and works of Jesus.*

*We thank you that when we are inspired by you, we can inspire others to live the lives that you intended them to live. Help us each day to lean on you, to draw upon your inspiration and to walk in the power of your wisdom, as we seek to see you Kingdom come on earth as it is in heaven. In Jesus name, Amen!*

*Staying inspired is something that you must commit to daily. There are no shortcuts to being inspired.*

# Chapter 5
# Staying Inspired

Being inspired is all well and good, but staying inspired is the key. I have been in leadership roles for over 30 years. During that time, there have been seasons when I would say I was inspired and others when my inspiration levels were less than what I would have desired. What I learnt is that inspiration wanes with time unless we take steps to ensure we stay inspired.

People are attracted to inspirational leaders. But if their inspiration dwindles, they will be attracted to whichever leader appears on their radar. Therefore, in life and leadership, you must do all you can, with God's help, to stay inspired and be inspirational in how you live and lead the people, organisations and ministries God has brought you to.

About 25 years into my leadership journey, I realised the importance and responsibility for staying inspired lay with me. The circumstances of life had drained me of inspiration that I once had. I had lost enthusiasm for the work I was doing and lost sight of the purpose God had for me. Over time, I recognised that staying inspired is a lifelong commitment of anyone who wants to have a positive influence on others.

It may seem an obvious statement, but the truth is you cannot inspire others if you are not inspired. A leader who stays inspired continues to encourage others.

We read in the Bible about the likes of Caleb who continue to believe anything is possible with God, despite their age.

Unlike most of the other spies who went into the land of Canaan, Caleb, who was in his 80s, came out with a faith-filled report. May you remain inspired to believe that, with God, all things are possible.

Whilst I am nowhere near as old as Caleb – I'm now in my mid-50s – I have had to learn to commit to staying inspired and to taking consistent, ongoing steps to ensure I continue to live life in a way that inspires others to be Jesus-centred. In that journey of commitment, I have identified seven keys that I want to share with you.

## 7 keys to staying inspired

### 1. Daily Practice

Staying inspired is something that you must commit to daily. There are no shortcuts to being inspired. Over the years, I am sure you have tried to take shortcuts. But the reality is that they rarely lead to good outcomes. God often designs lessons and experiences for us to take if we follow His path. He leads rather than trying to take shortcuts designed by man.

As a child, I was taught to read and pray every day. Perhaps you were, too. During my teenage years and early adulthood, these practices became something I felt *I had* to do to please God. Eventually, I stopped reading and praying each day.

It was only later in life, after seeing the folly of trying to be Jesus-centred without communing with Jesus, that I began to realise these daily practices were not something *I had* to do but something I needed to do. When I realised my true identity as a son of God, I began to realise that I needed to reserve time daily to read God's Word, listen to His still small voice and pray faith-filled prayers.

Today, I would encourage you to examine your daily practices and set aside quality time every day to read, listen and pray. As you do, you will find that you will receive a fresh supply of inspiration from the Father.

## 2. Intake

One of the most important statements I have ever heard is, "Your intake determines your output."

Whilst not a quote from the Bible, I believe the message the statement conveys is correct and in line with what we read in Scripture. To continue to be inspired, the level and quality of our inspiration is determined by our intake. What we allow to come into our lives through our eyes and ears.

In my experience, you can't give out what you haven't taken in. You cannot inspire others unless you are inspired yourself.

The person determining whether what you are taking in is inspiring you to live and lead like Jesus is you, and you alone. You have the remote control! What you look at and what you listen to shapes how you think.

We need to feed our hearts and minds with:

- The life, love and words of Jesus.

- The lives, love and word of inspiring brothers and sisters who speak faith-inspired words of wisdom, hope and expectation.
- Stories that inspire our faith rather than stories that reinforce our fears.

If you wish to stay inspired, you must invest your time in the people and things that cause you to believe and stop investing your time in the people and things that cause you to doubt.

Today, I would encourage you to reflect on your intake. Does your intake inspire you or do you need to filter out the images and voices that are draining you of inspiration?

Remember, whoever inspires you most sets the altitude at which you live and lead.

## 3. Focus

To stay inspired, you need to check your focus constantly. Experience tells me that the times when my focus has been firmly on Jesus are those when I was able to live and lead more like Jesus. They were also the times when I was most inspired.

Perhaps this is not a surprise given that Colossians 3:2 says, "Set your minds on things above, not on earthly things."

It is easy to be distracted by what is going on around you, but the Bible says that 'we are not of this world'. Therefore, you need to check your focus continually. I know that I often find myself being distracted by the circumstances of life and allow my mind to become fixated on the problems I face rather than focusing on the God I serve.

A long-time friend is often used by God to speak prophetically into the lives of many. Winnie has a way of knowing when I am 'off focus'. On many occasions, she has looked at me and said one word: 'FOCUS!'

Today I would say that if you wish to stay inspired, FOCUS on the things that are above. The Apostle Paul, in his letter to the Philippians, says it so much better than I can: "Finally, brothers and sisters, whatever is true, whatever is noble, whatever is right, whatever is pure, whatever is lovely, whatever is admirable – if anything is excellent or praiseworthy – think about such things."

## 4. Abiding

Where are you abiding? Abiding is an Old English adjective seldom used today. You are probably more familiar with the noun 'abode'. Rather than being asked where you live someone might ask, "Where is your abode?"

In the natural sense, our abode, or the place where we abide, is where we call 'home'. It is a place where we can relax, rest and be refreshed. It is where we can be who we are without pretending to be someone else.

The same is true in the spiritual sense. Your abode, or the place where you abide, is a place where you can relax, rest and be refreshed. It is where you can be the person God made you to be, not who Man thinks you should be. It is a place of freedom and a place where you can be inspired by your heavenly Father.

John 15:4 says, "Remain in me, as I also remain in you. No branch can bear fruit by itself; it must remain in the vine. Neither can you bear fruit unless you remain in me."

Staying inspired requires you to abide in the vine[5], which is the family God has grafted you into. You cannot flourish and produce good fruit if you are not abiding in Him. You cannot continue to be inspired if you do not remain part of the vine that God designed you to be part of.

As I write these words, I am reminded of an old song we sang in Sunday school called 'Abiding in the Vine'.[6] I believe that if we abide in the vine, we will be able to say:

*I've found a new way of living*
*I've a new life divine*
*I've got the fruit of the Spirit*
*I'm abiding, abiding in the vine*

*Abiding in the vine*
*Abiding in the vine*
*Love joy health peace*
*he has made them mine*
*I've got prosperity, power and victory*
*Abiding, abiding in the vine.*

---

[5] Abiding in the vine is how John 15:4 is expressed in some translations of the Bible

[6] https://www.lyricsmode.com/lyrics/p/pastor_earnest/abiding_in_the_vine.html

## 5. Rest

I have often heard people talk about 'resting in the Lord'; however, when I refer here to rest, I mean physical, emotional and spiritual rest, so our bodies, souls and minds become refreshed.

In 2009 and 2014, for differing reasons, I reached a place that many refer to as 'burnout'. The stresses and strains of business (2009) and ministry (2014) caused me to reach a place where I just had no more to give physically, emotionally and spiritually. In the first instance, there were times when I feared I was 'losing my mind'. In the second instance, my mind was so severely affected that I have little or no recollection of what happened over three months. It was as if my brain decided it had had enough.

When you are not getting enough rest, you do not function at your best. You lack the strength you would otherwise have, and your emotions become so entangled by the circumstances you face you are not likely to inspire others.

As a Jesus-centred leader, you cannot allow ourselves to reach that point. You need to follow the example of Jesus: He knew what it was to be under pressure and in; He knew how to withdraw from the crowds, enjoy the company of friends and how to sleep well, even in the middle of a storm.

If you want to stay inspired, you need to find ways to rest, otherwise you will become dried up by the heat of the circumstances you encounter and washed up by the storms face. To stay inspired you need to commit to finding time for rest.

My friend, Steve Brown is the President of Arrow Leadership in North America. He has developed a leadership health check in which he asks:

a) What are you daily habits for rest and renewal?
b) What are your weekly habits for rest and renewal?
c) What are your monthly habits for rest and renewal?

To stay inspired, perhaps you need to consider these questions.

## 6. Health and Well-being

How are you? No, I mean how are you *really*? If you have read this far in this book, you could be someone who knows how to give an answer that convinces most people that you are OK. But deep down, you know that you are not as healthy or as well as you could be.

In my mid-40s, I had a revelation of the nature and scale of God's call on the rest of my life. I knew that I was not physically fit and would need to get into shape to have the energy to do all that God was calling me to do. So, I took action! I lost a considerable amount of weight and got fit. For a couple of years, all was well: I had more energy; I could do more and keep going from 7 am to 11 pm. But as time passed, the discipline required to be healthy slipped. I gained weight, and my energy levels plummeted. I struggled to stay inspired as I did not have the energy. It became easier to sit in a chair and eat fast food.

I have learned that to stay inspired I need to do all I can to stay healthy and look after our well-being. When we are healthy in our bodies, our emotions are less likely to be bombarded with low self-worth. As a result, we are more likely to rise up into our true identity as sons and daughters of God.

Perhaps, today, God is saying that if you desire to live and lead like Jesus, you need to focus on your health and well-being so you can continue to be inspired and be all that God has called you to be.

As for me, I am just about to eat a piece of fruit and go for a walk.

## 7. Thin Places

The final key to staying inspired is to find your 'thin place.' No, I am not referring to your waistline, but those places where you find it easiest to connect with God to hear His voice and sense His presence.

A thin place has been described as 'a place where one can walk in two worlds – the worlds are fused together, knitted loosely where the differences can be discerned or tightly where the two worlds become one. A place not perceived with the five senses. Experiencing them goes beyond those limits'.[7]

Jesus had 'thin places' where He went to be alone with the Father. He knew the value of having a place where he could be alone with His Father and hear His voice without interruption.

---

[7] https://thinplacestour.com/what-are-thin-places/

During my first experience of chronic stress in 2009, I found my thin place. It was a place on the north coast of Northern Ireland, overlooking a two-mile-long beach. Every time I went, I sat on a seat facing out to sea and would hear God speak. It was as if there was an 'open heaven' over that spot. Over six months, I sensed God instruct me to be there every Monday morning. I still remember walking away from that thin place regularly texting my wife with what God had said to me as I sat there.

More recently, during the first Coronavirus lockdown in the UK, travel was not permitted beyond the immediate area near your home. I was frustrated! Lockdown regulations were preventing me getting to my thin place. God led me to a new thin place not far from home, overlooking the mountain on which St Patrick tended sheep when he first came to Ireland 1,600 years ago. I was there three times a week, sitting and listening to what God would say.

Wherever you find your thin place, you will find it is where God downloads fresh revelation to you that will fuel your inspiration.

### And finally...

Stay inspired! Divine inspiration will set you apart from the rest of the crowd.

*Communities are transformed when you are inspired to believe that the future can be better than the past.*

## Chapter 6
# Inspiring Others

The true purpose of staying inspired is so you might inspire others. It has been my experience that when people are inspired, they do great things. When they are not, they do not. The only way to see your world transformed is if people who are inspired by God inspire others.

If you look back in time, there will be people who stand out in your mind as being inspirational. You may recall a family member, teacher or Sunday school leader who inspired you. My earliest recollection of an inspiring person is a gentleman called Billy, who taught Bible class at our local church.

Billy had grown up in our village but did not let the small-mindedness of some stop him from being a schoolteacher. Nor did it stop him from excelling at the long jump and representing Ireland at the Commonwealth games. I remember thinking if he could achieve that there was nothing that could not be achieved with commitment and dedication.

Over the years, the role models you look towards or aspire to be should be those who encourage you to do great things. They should give you a sense of hope for a better tomorrow and remove any sense of not being good enough from your mind. That said, I wonder what type of role model you have become? Are you someone people look to for inspiration? Or someone who gives people hope and helps them believe that anything is possible?

Proverbs 27:17 says, "As iron sharpens iron, so a friend sharpens a friend." May we be the type of friends that people want to know because when they are in our company, they become 'sharper', in the sense that they become wiser and more inspired to be the best they can be.

John Quincy Adams the sixth President of the United States of America said: "If your actions inspire others to dream more, learn more, do more and become more, you are a leader."

As a Jesus-centred leader, it is your duty, before God, to inspire others to dream more, learn more, do more and become more. God-inspired inspiration can encourage ordinary people to become Jesus-centred leaders who will change the world. I have no doubt that communities are transformed when you are inspired to believe that the future can be better than the past.

## So how can you inspire others?

People are inspired through your action, words and deeds. Everything you say or do has the power to influence others if you intentionally set your focus on being inspiring people. Each day choose to speak words of faith, hope, love and affirmation and act in accordance with what you say.

There are several ways you can inspire others. As an aid to memory and learning, I have set these out as an acronym of the word **INSPIRE**!

## I - Identify Potential

Everyone is God's unique creation. God has imparted gifts and talents that are waiting to be brought to the surface and used to make the world a better place.

When you awaken to that revelation, you begin to see each person you meet as a goldmine of heaven-sent potential waiting to be mined. Through the presence of the Holy Spirit in your life, you can see in others what they cannot see in themselves: you can see the true value and purpose of their lives.

When you see people through the Holy Spirit's lens, you recognise that your role as a Jesus-centred leader is to help people identify their potential. Often, the potential has not yet been realised, or it may have become buried under the weight of choices or circumstance. Paul, writing to Timothy, had to remind him to stir up the gift that lay within him. Although Timothy was a young leader in his own right, he needed the voice of someone he trusted to call out of him the gifts and talents that God had placed within.

As someone called to inspire others, make it your mission, like the Apostle Paul, to identify people who cannot see the potential in themselves.

## N - Nurture Belief

Many of you reading this book will believe in God but may not believe in themselves. Self-doubt and self-deprecation have spread through the world like life-destroying cancer. While many believe in God, they doubt themselves and doubt the ability of God to work through them.

This issue might be due to the cultural or religious environment in which you grew up or the cultural or religious environment familiar to you.

I grew up in an environment where I was taught that humility meant doing what you were told and accepting the hand that life dealt you. Words were spoken over my life by well-meaning family members and leaders that made it hard to believe that I could become anything more than a son of two working-class, sick parents living on state benefits.

Your circumstances may have been different, but each person has experienced circumstances that have not been productive in nurturing belief. It is your role, as someone who lives and leads like Jesus, to nurture belief in those you meet and lead. One of my favourite verses of Scripture is 1 Thessalonians: 5-11, which says, "Therefore encourage one another and build each other up, just as in fact you are doing."

The Apostle Paul, writing to the Thessalonians, recognised that they were nurturing belief in each other. He was encouraging them to continue to encourage and build each other up. May you continue to do likewise.

## S - Speak Life

You may have sung the words of a rhyme that 'sticks and stones may break my bones, but names will never harm me' as a child. Let us make no mistake this is not true! Many of us live with painful memories of words spoken over us in our childhood — and even in more recent years. These words have had the power to impact our lives long after the pain of the physical wounds have gone. The psychological impact of words on our minds and emotions can either be life-controlling or life-empowering.

The Bible reaffirms this in Proverbs 18 which says, "Death and life are in the power of the tongue." The words we speak can either kill a person's dreams or can ignite a fire that will bring their dreams to life. Our role as Jesus-centred leaders should be to use our words to bring life to every person and situation we encounter.

What sets you apart from non-Christian leaders is that what you say can be filled with the life-giving truth of the Bible. They can be words that bring healing and release from the bondage that people have experienced due to the hurt and pain caused by the negative words of others.

You have the power to speak life, not just into individuals, but also families, businesses, organisations, communities and nations. You can inspire communities to believe that transformation is possible and inspire nations to believe that they can rise up out of the place of economic and social despair and become beacons of life-giving hope.

Wherever you go today, whoever you meet, speak life.

## P - Plan Expectantly

During the pandemic that swept the world in 2020, many people seemed to lose hope. In doing so, they also lost the ability to plan expectantly for the future. Planning for a future that cannot be seen is difficult, but it is even more challenging in a world where all we had known changed almost overnight.

Amid such a world, I began to sense that God was once again calling me, and those I have the privilege and honour to inspire, to be a person who would plan expectantly. Within my nation, God has blessed me with the opportunity to chair the national Youth for Christ movement. When I met with their leaders, six months into the pandemic, I sensed God ask me to inspire them to believe. The acronym in this chapter has its origins in the talk I gave that day. A key part of it was encouraging the leaders to plan expectantly.

To plan expectantly requires faith: faith to believe that when God says he has plans for us that His word can be trusted, and faith to believe that when God says He will give us hope and a future that He will do what he says. Inspiring those you lead to believe God has good plans is a vital ministry these days.

Plan expectantly and inspire others to plan expectantly.

## I - Identify Opportunities

Some of you will be old enough to remember Hughie Green hosting a television show in the UK called 'Opportunity Knocks'. The concept was quite simple: budding stars were invited to entertain a live audience and scored on their performance based on the 'Clapometer'. Many of the entertainers I remember as a youth found fame after appearing on 'Opportunity Knocks'.

As a Christian, I believe that opportunity knocks at our door each day. God has placed His wisdom within you. According to Proverbs 8, He births within you witty inventions. How amazing it is that the ability to identify opportunities is infused within you from heaven!

As you take time to tune your spirits to the voice of the Father, I believe that He can cause you to see opportunities that others cannot see, and He will give us faith to step into these opportunities so that the world can be a better place. Such is the Father's love for you and the world in which you live.

Jesus, when He was on this earth, saw opportunities that others did not see and as a result, took steps of faith that others would not take. I believe in these days God will reveal opportunities to His sons and daughters that will cause us to take steps of faith that others will not take. In doing so I believe that God will enable us to inspire other brothers and sisters, so that can they can identify opportunities that are reserved for those who seek the Lord.

## R - Release Inspirers

Are you a hoarder? Perhaps you like to keep things 'just in case you might need them, knowing that you probably will never use them again. Or, perhaps, you like holding on to things as they have sentimental value. The danger is that hoarding can become an obsession. If you have watched TV programmes about hoarding, you may have seen that it can have a negative impact on the physical and psychological health of the hoarder.

As leaders, when we find that God has blessed us with inspirational people on our team, there is a tendency to want to keep them to ourselves. We want to 'hoard' them so that we can use their inspiration for our business, organisation or ministry. But God may have brought that person of inspiration into your world for a specific purpose and season. God may want that person to and inspire another business, organisation or ministry. Letting go can be hard!

Perhaps God has placed a person of inspiration in your life. Be prepared, if God speaks, to let that person go. In releasing a person of inspiration, you can be assured you will reap a harvest of inspiration. You will also have the joy of seeing them being inspired and encouraged to impact the lives of so many more by sowing a person of inspiration into another business, organisation or ministry.

## E - Encourage Others

The final letter of the word 'inspire' is the letter 'e'. When I think of the letter 'e', I think of the word 'encourage', as I believe encouragement is the primary ministry that God has called me. Someone recently said that I should change my name on social media to 'Tommy The Encourager'. I am not so sure about that! But if, indeed when, I am promoted to glory that is the inscription on my gravestone, I will be happy.

This year, through the ministry of 'Christians Who Lead', 'The Encouragers' Network' will launch globally. The network is a worldwide movement that seeks to encourage people to believe that, with God, nothing is impossible. We believe networks of encouragers will spring up in every city and nation in the world who will commit to releasing one faith-filled word of encouragement each day of the year. Just think of the impact that could have globally!

I honestly believe that through words of faith-filled encouragement you can inspire people to believe in a great future. Will you join me?

Commit to encouraging others each day. You can start by encouraging a family member, a work colleague or a neighbour. Allow God to lead you to those He wants you to encourage. A lady I know has been led to encourage a different health care worker each day. Another man has been led to encourage a different business person each day as they seek to find a way through the economic uncertainties that we face.

Whatever you do, wherever you go, encourage one another.

## Inspiring others: an action plan

As I conclude this chapter and this section on inspiration, I would encourage you to take time to reflect on how you can inspire others. Set aside time, in God's presence, and ask Him to identify potential, nurture belief, speak life, plan expectantly, identify opportunities, release inspirers and encourage others. Record what God says in the table below and then use the table as an action plan to inspire others.

| | |
|---|---|
| I - Identify Potential | |
| N - Nurture Belief | |
| S - Speak Life | |
| P - Plan Expectantly | |
| I - Identify Opportunities | |
| R - Release Inspirers | |
| E - Encourage Others | |

# Section 3 : Impact

*Knowing you are a child of God changes how you approach life, and it will cause our impact in life to be so much greater.*

# Chapter 7
# **Impacting People**

From an early age, I had a desire to help other people. The desire may have come from having to be a carer to my mother and family during times of prolonged illness. As far back as I can remember, I would draw pictures of myself sitting behind a desk wearing a stethoscope, waiting to see my next patient.

While my childhood dream of being a doctor did not come to pass, God has led me on a path that has helped me diagnose difficulties in lives, organisations and communities and offer a 'prescription' of what can address the problems. For this, I am thankful to God. It has allowed me to have a positive impact on many people over the last 35-plus years.

As someone seeking to live and lead like Jesus, I believe that positively impacting lives should be central to all that you do. Through Jesus, you can impact lives in ways that those who do not trust Jesus cannot. You have been given unique gifts, talents and wisdom by God himself to allow you to positively impact the lives of people all over the world. Your greatest legacy will be the lives, organisations and communities you impact.

Whilst there are many factors that might affect the type and scale of impact you have, I believe there are four key determinants:

## 1. Identity Determines Impact

In the first three chapters of this book, I considered how our identity is formed, transformed and empowered. When you know that your identity has been shaped by Jesus and empowered by the Holy Spirit, then your impact can be so much greater than if you are struggling with a lack of identity and low self-worth.

*a) Your impact will be greater when we know who you are.*

Living and leading from a place of reassurance of who you are gives you confidence. As a result, you can live and lead knowing you are created for a purpose by God. You are not an accident; you are here through divine design.

*b) Your impact will be greater when you know whose you are*

Having a revelation that you are a son or daughter of God changes how you approach life. It enables you to live life through the lens of our Father rather than through your own eyes. Knowing you are a child of God changes how you approach life, and it will cause our impact in life to be so much greater.

*c) Your impact will be greater when you know who God says you are.*

A family friend from the 1980s used to sing an old chorus:

*"If I AM says I am, then I am who I AM says I am;*
*If I AM says I can do, then I can do what*
*I AM says I can do."*

Living from a place of knowing who the great I AM (God) says you are, then you can approach life and leadership with a God-confidence that will enable us to have significant impact on the lives of people.

*d) Your impact will be greater when you know you are secure in Him*

Insecurity hinders many people from becoming who God has called them to be. The enemy attacks our security, as he knows that when we are insecure, we do not have the impact we are designed to have. But when we are secure in who God has called us to be, knowing that He will never leave us or forsake us, then there is no limit to the impact God can cause us to have in this life.

## 2. Inspiration Determines Impact

In chapters four to six, I looked at how to be inspired, stay inspired and inspire others. Without a doubt, being an inspiration leads to impact. Rarely have I seen an uninspired person positively impact the lives of people. More often than not, they live mundane lives that fail to fulfil their true potential.

That is not the destiny of a Jesus-centred leader. God's plan for you is that you are inspired and stay inspired so you can continue each day to inspire others and have a positive impact on their lives. It is my observation that:

*a) Inspired people impact people each day (individual impact).*

Your impact can increase one life at a time if you choose to inspire at least one other person each day.

The impact of that individual may be small, or it may be life-changing. A lifetime spent inspiring one person each day means you can have a positive impact on thousands.

*b) Inspired people take actions that inspire others to take action (multiplier impact).*

When you are a person of inspiration, other people watch your actions to see if they can learn from you. When you take action, based on how God is inspiring you, there will be others who are inspired to take action themselves. In turn, that will lead to a positive impact on people that we may never know. Multiple impacts occur, meaning that our inspired actions can have an impact on the lives of tens of thousands.

*c) Inspired people inspire others to make changes that will have a long-term impact (lasting impact).*

Inspiration leads you to inspire others, and that inspiration will lead to the lives of people, families, communities and even whole nations being positively impacted for many years. When you live life inspired by God, I believe your impact will have a lasting impact. It will bring hope to people even after our time on earth has ended.

## 3. Character Determines Your Impact

The third determinant of impact, and perhaps one of the most commonly discussed, is your character. Having a good character will ensure that you have an ongoing opportunity to impact others positively. If your character is flawed, then the impact of your life is significantly reduced. As a result, you must remain Jesus-centred so that you can live and lead in a manner that allows you to have the maximum level of positive impact on people's lives.

Without doubt, your impact will be directly proportional to the quality of your character.

To help you consider various aspects of your character that you need to seek to align daily with God's ways, I have set out below an acronym of the word 'character'. As you consider each of these aspects of character, it is my prayer that the Holy Spirit guides you as to which aspects of your character you need to focus on so you continue to positively impact lives for many years to come.

- **Consistent.** To impact more lives, more deeply you need to live and lead with consistency. In your private, family, church and public life, you must be seen to be consistent at all times, otherwise people will lose faith in you and you lose the ability to have a positive impact.

- **Honest.** When you appoint people to a position of responsibility, always seek to ensure that they are honest people. You would not want to have someone representing you who was less than honest. Likewise, you are representing God and are an ambassador of His Kingdom. In all your transactions in life, seen or unseen, your impact will be greater if you are honest in all things.

- **Approachable.** You, like me, will know some people who appear 'unapproachable.' There is no way that you would even think about approaching them for advice or guidance. These people can have little or no positive impact on your life due to their unapproachability. However, you are a follower of Jesus, who was approachable and accessible to all, unless spending time alone with His Father. May you be likewise.

- **Real.** If you want to have a positive impact on the lives of people then you have got be real. Too often, we see people giving the impression that they are something they are not; they do not appear to be genuine! If you want to maximise impact, then you need to appear genuine to people. Too often, in Christian circles, leaders have appeared so super-spiritual that ordinary people could not relate to them. <u>Be real! People will relate to you better.</u>

- **Attentive.** People want to feel that they are being listened to and heard. As a Jesus-centred person, you need to be sure that you take time to be attentive to what people say. You need to avoid the tendency to become so busy that you do not have time to hear from the Father or to hear from the people the Father would have us help. Being attentive leads to better understanding, which leads to greater impact.

- **Clear.** Clarity in what you are doing, saying and asking people to do is critical to having impact. If people think 'he hasn't got a clue what he's doing', or 'I haven't got a clue what he's trying to say', then there is little chance of making a positive impact. If you are not clear in what you are asking people to do, you cannot expect their actions to have the impact you desire. I pray that the Holy Spirit helps you to have greater clarity in what you do and say.

- **Trustworthy.** To impact the lives of people positively, they need to feel they can trust you. In the same way that God impacts our lives, as you come to the point of realisation that you can trust Him, others need to feel that they can trust you. That means that you need to do what you have promised; always show up when you say you will. Forming trustworthy bonds with people increases your level of impact and effectiveness.

- **Encouraging.** The level of impact you have on lives is determined by the level of encouragement you provide. People can do great things but often do not because they lack encouragement. I believe that as you purposely commit to speaking words of encouragement over lives, you will see the level of the positive impact that you have on those lives significantly increase.

- **Relevant.** If people do not see you as being relevant to their situation or the context in which they live, you are likely to have little or no impact on their lives. One way of appearing relevant is to share your own life's challenges with the people you are seeking to impact. Show them how, with God's help, you overcame challenges similar to those they may be facing. That way, you are more likely to appear relevant and, in doing so, will have a significant impact on their lives.

## 4. Relationships Determine Impact

The final determinant of impact is the importance of relationships. Matt Bird, a Christian speaker, author and businessman, says, "Relationships are the currency of life and business."

In other words, every transaction in life is dependent on the quality of relationships. Everything we seek to do requires relationships, they are central to the extent to which we can impact lives positively. The nature and quality of the relationships you have affects the nature and quality of your life, and the nature and quality of the impact you have. To increase your impact, you need to spend time cultivating and developing relationships with like-minded people and those with whom God would have you impact.

In New Testament times, Jesus formed many relationships on many levels. However, He developed three core relationships:

a) Relationship with His Father

b) Relationship with His team (disciples and friends)

c) Relationship with those He impacted (both religious and irreligious)

To ensure the impact you were designed to achieve, you need to:

- Deepen your relationship with God;

- Grow in relationship with those who God has or is drawing alongside you;

- Develop relational connections to those God is calling you to impact.

Investing in relationships pays dividends in terms of the impact you have. In my experience, the level of impact you have depends on the strength of relationships you form and the relationships you are led to form by God. He will open doors to you so you can impact people you do not yet know.

## And finally...

Take some time to ask God to help you become:

- Confident in who you are.
- Confident in being a child of God.
- Confident in who God says you are.
- Confident in who He has called you to be.
- Inspired by Him so you can inspire others.
- Strong in character so that your impact can be lasting.
- Committed to growing in relationship with God, those God calls to help you and those God calls you to impact.

## Prayer

*Father, I pray that everyone reading these words will grow in confidence in who they are in you. I pray they will be inspired by you and inspire others, and that they will be strong in character, strengthened by the power of the Spirit. I pray that they will grow in their relationship with you, with their brothers and sisters in the faith, and in relationship with those you have called them to reach.*

*In Jesus name I pray. Amen.*

*Leadership is more about posture than position.*

# Chapter 8
# Impacting Organisations

Every day you are blessed with the opportunity to engage with organisations where you have influence. The type of influence you have will either be positive or negative, dependent on how you approach the opportunities God affords you.

Whether you are a volunteer, an employee, a CEO or a board member, you have the opportunity to have an impact on organisations daily. As someone who lives and leads like Jesus, your desire should be to impact those organisations positively, so the lives of those in the organisation and those affected by it see Christ's reflection in all you say and do.

Looking at my life, I believe the impact I have had on the organisations I have engaged with has been largely positive. There are, of course, things I could have done so much better and, perhaps, others I should not have done. Whether it be in the voluntary sector, public sector, business or church, we all have opportunity to impact organisations in a positive and Jesus-like manner.

To help you grow the positive impact on the organisations in your circle of influence, I have set out several ways you can positively impact them, regardless of the level you are engaged with them.

## Leading from the bottom up

The term 'leading from the bottom up' may be new to some. But I have found it helps people understand that leadership is more about posture than position. You do not need to be a CEO in an organisation to be a leader. You can lead each day at the level at which you engage with that organisation. Do not see yourself as 'only a volunteer' or just 'a cog in a wheel'; see yourself as a child of God who can lead from whatever place of influence He has given you.

You may be asking, "How do I do that?"

I believe that there are three ways in which you can lead from the bottom, and this will positively impact charities, companies and churches without being in a so-called 'position of power'.

## 1. Lead by character

Competence and experience may open the door to an organisation for many people. But it is your character that determines the effect you have on it. As a believer in Jesus Christ, your character needs to demonstrate integrity, kindness, sincerity, self-control and generosity. If other team members see your positive characteristics, you are more likely to show leadership to your peers; you will be less likely to be adversely impacted by the negative influences of peers with fewer Christ-like characteristics.

By being consistently upright in all you do and say, you create an open door through which you will have opportunities to positively impact those with whom you work or serve.

## 2. Lead by example

As an employee or volunteer, you can increase the impact you have by leading by example. You should set a positive example for other team members.

My son recently told me about a friend who had a new job but was under surveillance by his bosses as they did not believe he was doing what he was asked to do. He was setting was seen to be a bad example and negatively impacting the behaviour of other employees. Some were heard to say, "If he can get away with it so can we!"

I wonder what people say about the example you set. I pray, that as others look at your example, they are inspired to follow it because it honours the employer and honours other members of staff or the volunteer team.

Setting a good example helps you have an increased impact on those with whom you work or serve. It also helps the organisation have a more positive impact in fulfilling its goals, which opens doors and promotion opportunities to you.

## 3. Lead by commitment

In the digital, fast-paced world in which we live, it is increasingly rare to find people with a long-term commitment to what they are doing. People often move on as soon as a better opportunity arises or once someone says something they did not want to hear.

Positive impact in any organisation grows over time. In my experience, the longer you remain committed to bringing a positive influence to a charity, company or church, the more likely you are at having a greater impact. There will, of course, be hurdles and roadblocks along the way, but with a positive, Christ-like attitude, you are likely to continue to positively impact fellow team members and the organisation with a determined commitment to be a transformative presence.

It is my prayer that with God's strength and grace you can lead from the bottom through leading by character, example and commitment.

## Leading from the top

For those of us who have been blessed with the opportunity 'to lead from the top', we need to constantly remind ourselves that we hold a position that can positively impact many lives. This includes those within the organisation and the wider circle of influence that the organisation has with its suppliers, customers, clients, members or beneficiaries. Whether you are the CEO, department leader or section manager of a business, a charity or a church, you have an exponential ability to positively impact the organisation and all who work, serve or engage with it.

To do so, I believe your impact can be greater if you lead with vision, integrity and compassion.

### 1. Lead with vision

Jon Gordon, the Florida based leadership coach, says, "Great leaders share their belief, vision, purpose and passion with others and in the process, they inspire others to believe, act and impact."

Over my 35-plus years of work, ministry and leadership, I have been privileged to meet a few leaders whom I would regard as being in the 'great' category. All were visionary men and women of belief, purpose and passion, and all were people who inspired others to believe, act and impact.

The need to lead with vision is abundantly clear in the Bible. Proverbs 29:18 tell us, "Where there is no vision, the people perish."[8] Joel 2 tells us, "Write the vision, make it clear."

To increase the impact on the organisation you lead, or help lead, you need to be a man or woman of vision. You need to have a clear picture of where God wants you to lead the organisation so that those you lead are clear on where it is going. Only when doing so can those who work for or serve the organisation make their best contribution to its impact.

If you lead with a clear vision, you create a multiplier effect in terms of the positive impact each team member brings to the organisation and the people it impacts or serves. Team members become focused and remain energised if they can see where the organisation is heading and if they can see how what they are doing is helping to achieve a positive outcome.

## 2. Lead with integrity

You can be highly successful as a volunteer, employee and leader, but if you do not have integrity the positive

---

[8] King James Version

impact you have will eventually erode. That is not a scenario we ever wish to find ourselves in as leaders.

If I ask you to identify leaders who have lost impact and influence because of a lack of integrity, I suspect you would be able to name quite a few. In recent times, the Christian world has been rocked by hearing accounts where leaders who they thought to be men and women of integrity, have not lived up to the standards they would have expected of a Christian leader.

May you seek at all time to walk with integrity, speaking and acting as Jesus-centred son or daughter of God, so your impact may be positive now and remain so for however many years God blesses you to live on this earth.

### 3. Lead with compassion

If you want to achieve the best results from a team and, in turn, help an organisation have the maximum positive impact, you need to determine, like Jesus, to lead with compassion.

Compassionate leadership is the type of leadership that motivates people to go out of their way to help the physical, spiritual or emotional hurts or pains of others. Whether that is in your family, community, workplace or church, I believe God desires that we lead with full consideration of the physical, emotional and spiritual dimension of each person we lead and of each person our organisation seeks to impact. Employees and volunteers should never be considered objects that help us achieve an outcome. They are people who God loves, within whom He has placed unique gifts and talents, and those who God has entrusted us to lead in a manner that enables them to live out their full potential.

In leading with this type of compassion, you can enable your teams and organisations to have a God-sized impact.

## Leading from the board

You may have reached a stage in life where God has opened up opportunities for you to serve on the board of organisations. These are both positions of responsibility and honour. Legally, there are duties you need to fulfil to comply with company, corporate or charitable law. Whilst these may considered a burden, I believe the opportunities being a board member brings far outweighs the weight of responsibility.

I have recently been appointed to and asked to chair boards of local, nation and international organisations. Each brings with it its own set of challenges and opportunities. The key determinant to how much positive impact you have on the organisations you have the honour to help govern will be determined by how you lead. From my observations, I believe that board members can maximise the impact they bring to a charity, company or church when they seek to lead in three specific ways:

### 1. Lead by enabling

As board members, it is our role to ensure the organisation develops, grows and maximises its influence through accountable governance and sound leadership. As individual board members, we can play a significant role in this by leading in a way that seeks to enable, not hinder, the board, the CEO and the staff/volunteer team to fulfil their roles to the best of their abilities. It may mean we have to set aside our agendas and methods to encourage the corporate, collective body to maximise its impact. Board members who lead by enabling contribute to the life of the organisation beyond participation in board meetings. Their engagement is always empowering, not controlling.

## 2. Lead by supporting

Since taking the role of Chair of Youth for Christ and of the Bible Society in my nation, I have started to see more clearly the need for board chairs and members to support the work of the organisation and, in particular, the CEO and their team.

In practical ways, this may mean that, as board members, we help grow the impact of the organisation through the investment of our funds, enabling new opportunities to be taken or through the investment of our time.

After I complete the writing of this chapter, I will join the monthly online prayer meeting of the Bible Society. This is not just because it is the right thing for me to do as the Chair, but I know my presence will be seen as an expression of support for the initiative that the CEO has taken and as support for the staff team.

Whatever you can do to support the organisations and staff/volunteers of the organisations you are on the board of, seek to do so in a manner that shows the love of Jesus.

### 3. Lead by encouraging

Encouragement is one of the greatest gifts we can give to the world. Earlier in this book, I referred to Thessalonians in which it says that we are to encourage one another. Without a doubt, the boards, staff and volunteers of the organisation you lead needs encouragement. Through that encouragement, I believe their impact can be greater.

I would encourage you to determine that you will do at least one thing as a board member to encourage the team that leads and serves the organisation you help to govern. In doing so, I believe that the team members and the organisation will have a greater impact and that you will reap a harvest from seeds of encouragement you have sown that, in turn, will help you become more impactful in what you do in life.

## And finally...

## Growing Your Impact Indicator

In the Impact Indicator below, reflectively and honestly score the level of impact you currently believe you have, where 0 is no impact and 10 is the maximum. For each area of impact, write down what you plan to do to grow the positive impact you can have in the organisations in which you engage.

| Area of Impact | Level of Current Impact | How you plan to grow the positive impact you have |
| --- | --- | --- |
| Lead by character | | |
| Lead by example | | |
| Lead by commitment | | |
| Lead with vision | | |
| Lead with integrity | | |
| Lead with compassion | | |
| Lead by enabling | | |
| Lead by supporting | | |
| Lead by encouraging | | |

*The love of Jesus needs to continue to shine into communities long after the temporal fixes of man have faded away.*

## Chapter 9
# Impacting Communities

Jesus came to bring transformation that not only impacts the lives of individuals and organisations but entire communities.

When I was a consultant working with communities in post-conflict Northern Ireland, the word 'transformation' was regularly used. It described what was required to move communities from a conflict mentality to a post-conflict mentality. It indicated the need for a change of hearts and minds, away from the ways of the past to ways of peace and prosperity.

As you seek to live and lead like Jesus, I believe God will give you opportunities to impact communities so they can transition from those held captive to fear and defeat to those released to walk in faith and freedom. It is His desire to see His kingdom come in communities all over your nation and across the nations of the world. There is no community that cannot be transformed when it is impacted by Jesus-centred people, dedicated to following the ways of Christ.

I have observed and watched individuals, organisations, churches and Christian charities seek to bring transformational change to communities. From my observations and reading of the Bible, I have identified ten keys to impacting communities. I do not believe these are only the keys. But if we aspire to use them, God will open up the doors of communities to us so they can be transformed through the power of the Holy Spirit and His name is glorified.

# 10 Keys to Impacting Communities

## 1. Love unconditionally

Over many years, I had the honour of working with communities across Northern Ireland who were deeply impacted by conflict. Many of the leaders in these communities were suspicious of the motives of people who desired to help them. Often, their language and actions reflected those of people who were carrying the pain and hurt of the past.

As you seek to impact communities through Jesus-centred actions, you will also find people who react from the hurt of the past and will be less than easy to love. Whilst some will be turned off by the reaction of those they are trying to reach, it is good to remember their attitude towards you is less about you and more about their experiences.

In Jesus, we have the greatest model of unconditional love: loving people who seem impossible to love. At the Cross, referring to the soldiers who crucified him, Jesus said, "Father forgive them for they know not what they do." Regardless of what people have done or what they may do, God will give you the strength and compassion to love them. It is only when people who are not used to being loved unconditionally experience that kind of love that they become open to engaging and listening to what you have to say.

## 2. Develop relationships

If you do not have an established relationship with an individual, organisation or community, it is extremely hard to impact them. To impact communities, you need to take the time to develop relationships with that community.

Communities need to know that you have a genuine interest in them if they are to be open to the message we share with them. This thought reminds me of a pastor friend who kept a little book in the glove compartment of his car. Every time he met someone – be it in church, the community or their home – he would ask about their hobbies, passions, family members and even their pets. He would go to his car and make a note of what he had learnt. The next time he had an opportunity to visit anyone in the congregation, he would check his notebook before going to the house. Parishioners often reported how impressed they were that he remembered the names of their children, grandchildren and pets.

Pastor Johnny was not wasting time making notes he was investing time in building relationships that can lead to personal and community transformation. So, too, should you if you wish to see communities impacted. You need to take the time to invest in building relationships. It means sowing seeds of time, but the harvest you will see will be lives, families and communities impacted by the love of Jesus.

## 3. Commit long term

Short term interventions rarely bring long term change.

If you want to see generational change in a community, you need to be committed to long term engagement with it. One of my former pastors said that unless community teams were committed to showing up each week in a community for five years, there was little point in showing up at all.

'Fly by night' outreaches, evangelism and compassion programmes may have some degree of impact. But communities watch to see if the Church will be like other support agencies that move into communities when they are in crisis, then pull out just as quickly. Whichever community you wish to impact, you need to realise your commitment to that community cannot be short term. It must be long term. <u>The love of Jesus needs to continue to shine into communities long after the temporal fixes of man have faded away</u>.

May God help you to be ever present in the communities you are seeking to impact, always available to help those in need and always allowing God's love to shine.

## 4. Encourage continually

Over the years, I have done a fair amount of work in deprived communities in inner-city Belfast. These are communities identifiable by the scars of community conflict, societal division and generational unemployment. A quick fix is not going to have any lasting impact on communities like these.

If you had grown up in a community where it was common for your father, grandfather and every other adult in your family to be unemployed, it would take a lot of positive motivation and encouragement to see any hope of a different type of future. Within communities of this nature, there are very few voices of encouragement.

As you seek to live and lead like Jesus, you can be the voice of hope in communities where there is none. You can speak words of encouragement to children who do not receive encouragement at home. You can speak words of encouragement to young people with no prospects of employment. You can encourage single parents struggling to survive and men struggling with life-controlling issues. You can speak words of encouragement to business owners barely able to keep their doors open.

The words of encouragement you speak today release fresh hope for a better tomorrow.

## 5. Build trust

Trust is a precious commodity that is hard to gain and easy to lose. When trust is lost in individuals, organisations or churches, it is difficult to regain it. If people believe they cannot trust you, then nothing you say or do will have the desired impact.

In my work, I have often heard community leaders ask, "How do we know we can trust you?" Their starting point is not to trust anyone because they have had a lifetime of being let down. They have sometimes, sadly, been let down by the Church. They do not want to suffer the hurt of disappointment again, so they have built up defence mechanisms that need overcoming to build trust with them.

Trust is built a step at a time. Each time you promise to do something, the community will be watching to see if you do what you say you promise. They will judge your trustworthiness on whether they perceive you are a person of your word and whether you are a person of integrity, living a life that sets us apart from those who have sought to win the hearts of that community in the past but let them down.

Consistency, faithfulness and integrity are the foundations on which we build trust.

## 6. Meet needs

John C Maxwell, the American preacher and leadership guru, often quotes the famous words, "People don't care how much you know until they know how much you care."

You cannot expect people to listen to your message about Jesus unless you first demonstrate the love of Jesus. Where I grew up, we would have said, "You need to scratch where it itches." In other words, you need to be able to meet the needs of people if you want to transform the lives of people. For many, the 'here and now' needs they face are blinding them from the much greater eternal need they have of Jesus.

Traditional 'fire and brimstone preaching may have reached some, but most were not reached through fear-instilling sermons. People can be reached through hope-inspiring actions, however. During the recent coronavirus pandemic, this was evident. The Church stepped up to the mark across many nations and met the practical needs of people experiencing a lack of food, hope and a lack of community.

Meeting needs is essential, but it should never be considered the main role of the Church. It should, however, be one part of a multi-faceted approach to impacting communities that Jesus-centred individuals, groups and churches need to deploy.

## 7. Partner with others

Globally, there have been many studies about the principles and practices of what is regarded as 'community development'. It is widely accepted that there are four common levels at which community development practitioners have engaged with communities.

Level 1: Doing things *to* communities

Level 2: Doing things *for* communities

Level 3: Doing things *with* communities

Level 4: Doing things that help communities do things for themselves

Social scientists suggest that when seeking to do things 'to communities' barriers of resistance are created they feel something is being imposed upon them. When seeking to do something for a community, it will, at first, be accepting, but it soon becomes frustrated that it is not able to do things for itself.

Too often, in my experience, the Church has sought to do things to communities and do things for communities. However, evidence suggests that you see greater impact when you do things with communities and when you empower communities to do things for themselves.

If you want to see communities impacted with the love of Jesus, then you need to find ways of coming alongside communities, partnering with them, to see positive transformational change.

## 8. Inspire Confidence

The communities we seek to impact are often communities where there are low levels of confidence, often populated by people who, due to their circumstances, have little or no confidence in themselves or others. If such communities are to be transformed to become confident about their future, they need to regain belief in their abilities and the ability to overcome the challenges they face. They need to be inspired to see challenges as opportunities.

Your role as a Jesus-centred leader is to speak words of affirmation and belief into communities that have been bombarded with voices of condemnation and doubt. Jesus recognised this in the communities he visited during his years of ministry. He saw a sense of despair in the people he ministered to. His antidote for this despair was to ignite fresh hope in the lives of those who heard him speak. He inspired confidence in them to believe that through Him, all things are possible. And He told those who followed Him that they had each been given faith that can move mountains.

Make it your job to speak words that inspire confidence over the places where you live, work and minister, knowing that as you do, you will inspire confidence in people to believe for the greater things that are yet to come.

## 9. Empower Leaders

The older I get, the more I see what needs to be done. However, I also realise that I cannot even begin to scratch the surface of what needs to be done to impact communities.

The opportunities that God presents as you focus your eyes on Jesus will always exceed the capacity you have to seize them on your own. That is how God works! He wants you to realise that you cannot fulfil all that he has put in your heart on your own. He wants you to draw upon His strength, wisdom and grace, and He wants you to empower others to do what He would have you do.

Jesus showed how this works when training up the 12 disciples. He empowered them to do what the Father had called Him to do. He realised that His time was limited but that if He could empower others, the work would continue long after He was gone.

Perhaps you, like me, are now in the second half of your life, work and ministry. Now is a good time for you to begin developing and empowering others. Or perhaps you are a young leader; do not make the mistake of many who have gone before, trying to do it all on your own. You can achieve so much more when you empower others to lead, multiplying your impact on the communities God has called you to reach.

## 10. Celebrate transformation

It's always good to celebrate. Every accomplishment should be celebrated.

When seeking to transform communities through living and leading like Jesus, it is important to celebrate even the smallest signs of change. It encourages your teams to continue and those who have accomplished something they have never done so before. It spreads hope through the community that change is possible.

In all that you do to impact communities, it is important to celebrate God's faithfulness and recognise He is the true source of hope, which breaks through the darkness of the communities. When His name is praised, He responds by giving us opportunities to see His Kingdom come on earth as it is in heaven.

Whichever community you are seeking to impact, I pray that as you step out in faith, you will see God's kingdom come in that community as it is in heaven.

In summary, let us be those who:

- Love unconditionally
- Develop relationships
- Commit long term
- Encourage continually
- Build trust
- Meet needs
- Partner with others
- Inspire Confidence
- Empower Leaders
- Celebrate transformation

# Section 4 : Influence

*Influence grows over time
but can be lost overnight*

# Chapter 10
# Growing Influence

As you develop in your identity as a son or daughter of God, you begin to work under the inspiration of the Holy Spirit and your impact on lives, organisations and communities increases. It becomes evident to those around you, and people may say that you have influence.

In this chapter, I will look at what it means to grow in influence and consider the role of seven factors in the development of influence over time. In the final two chapters, I will look at how to steward the influence that God has given you and how that influence can be used to shape generations yet to come.

## Positional and Postural Influence

Cast your mind back to your childhood and you will recall individuals who influenced your life, largely due to the position they held in the community. They had the power to influence people's lives, decisions and, in some cases destiny, due to the power of the position they held.

In the 1970s, Cullybackey, where I grew up, three men held prominent positions in the village. Each influenced the village due to the position they held.

Firstly, there was Ernie Watt, the long-time principal of the local primary school. Both in the school context and the wider community, he was seen as a man of influence.

Then there was the Rev Hook, the local Presbyterian minister; he was the minister of the largest church in the village and had been in his role for the longest period.

Finally, there was Sergeant Boyle. His title, position and reputation kept even the most rebellious teenagers in order.

Each of the three gentlemen had positional influence. However, in this chapter, my focus will be less on positional influence and more on postural influence. Postural influence develops over time, not due to the position we hold, but due to the posture we take in life. CH Spurgeon, the famous 19th-century Baptist minister once said: "The serene, silent beauty of a holy life is the most powerful influence in the world, next to the might of the Spirit of God."

It is my prayer that as you grow in identity, inspiration and impact, you will continue to live a holy life that enables you to bring Godly influence on the nations of the world.

I believe that you can grow in influence if you remain centred on Jesus. In doing so, I believe that a range of factors plays a role. Some of these factors include the role of:

- Faithfulness
- Faith
- Fruitfulness
- Favour
- Focus
- Friends
- Foresight
- Finances

## • **The Role of Faithfulness**

George Washington is quoted as saying, "Example, whether it be good or bad, has a powerful influence."

Each day in life you set an example: to your family, friends, work colleagues and community. People are watching you whether or not you know. Each day people assess the type of character you have and the long-term cumulative effect of what will determine the influence you have.

As a result, I believe your faithfulness to God and the roles He has given you determines whether or not you become influential. If you are not faithful to the Word of God, you are not likely to be faithful to the work that God has called you to in the public sphere, the workplace or the church. Influence is a privilege that you need to respect. Influence grows over time but can be lost overnight. So, faithfulness has a central role in growing and maintaining influence.

When people observe that you are faithful to what you do, you begin to be regarded as being reliable, dependable and trustworthy. Each of these is stepping stones on the pathway to a life of influence.

- **The Role of Fruitfulness**

Each of us has been created to bear fruit. God has designed us to be fruitful in all that we do. Whilst godly influence is not focused on productivity, the extent of your fruitfulness in your work or ministry will determine the level of influence you have in the spheres in which you engage.

Jesus, in the Gospels, communicates several stories in which blessing is bestowed on those who are fruitful with their time, money and influence. As you walk with the

Lord, it should be your desire to be fruitful in all that you do.

Consequently, people will begin to take note of the results you achieve, and you will be rewarded with new and greater opportunities to demonstrate your fruitfulness. Each opportunity allows you to grow in influence, not just for the sake of influence, but so you have the ability to live and lead like Jesus in the shop, factory, office, or wherever God leads you to.

## • The Role of Focus

As you journey through life, you need to remain focused lest you become distracted by the temptations that can come with influence. *Influence needs to be Jesus-centred lest it becomes self-centred.* Sadly, too many Christian leaders have fallen into the trap of thinking it was all about them rather than maintaining their focus on bringing glory to Jesus.

Rick Warren, pastor and author of 'The Purpose Driven Life', suggests that, "The purpose of influence is to speak up for those who have no influence. Each day it is good to remind ourselves that we do not seek influence for our own sake but rather we seek influence so that we can bring positive transformational change to the lives of others."

While your focus stays on Jesus and the purpose to which he has called you, then your focus will be upward and outward rather than inward. Failure to do so will eventually lead to a demise in influence due to your moral weaknesses. You cannot and should not seek to live and lead without renewing focus on Jesus daily.

- **The Role of Foresight**

You may have heard that hindsight is a wonderful thing, however, I believe that foresight is an even more wonderful thing! It is one thing to be able to look back and say, 'If we had known we would have done things differently.' But it is so much better to be able to look forward and say, 'Let us do it this way so we can avoid the pitfalls that others experience.'

I believe God can supernaturally enable you, as His son or daughter, to see things others cannot. As you rest in His presence, I believe He can reveal to you the way that you are to go, the things that you are to do and the words you are to say. I like to call this the 'divine advantage'.

Regardless of the sector in which you work and lead, do not minimise the role that foresight can have. It can set you apart from others and advance you faster and further down the road than your colleagues or competitors. Time spent in prayer and the presence of God is not time off. It is an essential part of your work. It is a vital part of your preparation and a key component in the development of a life of Jesus-centred influence.

- **The Role of Faith**

As a believer in Jesus Christ, your faith has an undeniable role in the extent to which you grow in influence – or not. In Hebrews chapter 11, there are examples of people of great faith. In the early part of the chapter, verse six, the writer to the Hebrews says, "Without faith, it is impossible to please God because anyone who comes to him must believe that he exists and that he rewards those who earnestly seek him."

If, and I trust it is, your desire to please God, then you must operate out of the place of belief in Him. Not only do you see that is pleasing to God, but you learn that God rewards those who seek Him. Our faith in God will lead us to experience rewards that others who do not believe in God cannot receive. Your faith sets you apart from the crowd. It will cause you to take steps of faith, whilst others are held captive to fear.

God has given to each of us, His sons and daughters, a mustard seed of faith that we can choose to use in every realm of life. As you step out in faith, your confidence in God and His faithfulness grows. This gives you the ability to live and lead like Jesus at whatever level of life God positions you, causing you to grow in influence.

- **The Role of Favour**

Earlier in this book, I looked at the difference God's favour can make in our lives. Without a doubt, it can help you to achieve so much that others, perhaps wiser than you, would not be able to achieve.

It has been said that 'the favour of man can open doors, but the favour of God can move mountains'. I think I know which favour I would prefer!

Back in my early years of Christian ministry, I would be invited to speak in churches on a Sunday from time to time. A friend who had trained in pastoral ministry at the same time seemed to be getting more speaking opportunities than I was. It bothered me enough that I asked him how it was he was getting so many opportunities. He said that if the door did not open, he would kick it down. That may have worked for a time, but his opportunities were short-lived. The truth is that it is better to walk through doors that God opens through His favour, rather than try to open them yourself or convince others to open them for you. The doors that God opens through His favour will lead you to places where His grace can sustain you.

God's favour will take you places where He wants His influence to be released through His sons and daughters.

- **The Role of Friends**

Friends have a key role to play in determining the extent to which we grow in influence. Friends can either drag you down or lift you. It is perhaps stated more strongly in the words of Solomon in Proverbs 13:20: "Walk with the wise and become wise, for a companion of fools suffers harm."

Over the years I have found that friends shape your:

a) Thinking
b) Actions
c) Character
d) Destiny

Depending on who you choose as friends, you can either develop helpful thought patterns or self-destructive ones. They will either act in a Jesus-centred manner or a self-centred manner; develop a character of integrity or one that is dishonest and divisive; become a person of Godly influence or one who fails to fulfil the destiny God has birthed with us.

Choosing friends who live and lead like Jesus is critical to the development of Jesus-centred influence. Beyond that circle of friends, you may choose to have 'acquaintances', those you know and are friendly with but do not allow to shape who you are or who you become. Through our association with them, we seek to display to them the love of Jesus.

### • The Role of Finances

Finance is a subject that few like to discuss, but no one can avoid. Even the very mention of the word 'finances' on a list may disturb some. However, we cannot ignore the role that finances have in the development and growth of influence.

In everyday life, we hear people say that money talks, and so it does. But the real question is, 'What is money saying?'

For centuries, if not millennia, people have sought to use money to gain influence: either their money or the money of others. Some have sought to buy their way into positions of power and influence, while others have sought to use money to see a particular cause or ideology become more influential. Money can be used to gain influence for the good of mankind or to gain influence that brings people into bondage and captivity.

God-given influence, however, is a power that money cannot buy. It is something that comes from God alone. I believe that in releasing influence on His sons and daughters, God looks upon our hearts regarding our attitude towards money. He wants to determine whether you are driven by a desire for influence to have more finances or driven by a desire for influence so you can see lives, communities and nations transformed. I believe God wants to see whether you are prepared to sow money into the dreams and hopes He has placed in your life or whether you do not want to let go of the financial seeds He has placed within your hands.

As you grow in his likeness, I believe you will grow in your desire to steward your finances wisely and in your desire to sow finances into the work that God is doing through us and others.

## And finally...

As we live and lead like Jesus, we will grow in influence. Remember that influence is given by God for his purposes.

I would invite you to spend time in God's presence reflecting on these questions:

1. What is God wishing to say to me about faithfulness?
2. What is God wishing to say to me about fruitfulness?
3. What is God wishing to say to me about focus?
4. What is God wishing to say to me about foresight?
5. What is God wishing to say to me about faith?
6. What is God wishing to say to me about favour?
7. What is God wishing to say to me about friends?
8. What is God wishing to say to me about finances?

May God help you respond to His still small voice and become more like Him each day, so you grow in influence and bring Jesus-centred transformation to the lives of many.

*God's plan was never that we would use our influence to control people but rather that we use it to empower people*

# Chapter 11
# Stewarding Influence

Clint Eastwood, the actor and director, said, "It takes tremendous discipline to control the influence, the power you have over other people's lives."

What Clint discovered is even more true for those of us who live and lead like Jesus. The place of leadership, and the influence that it brings, can become a trap that the enemy uses to ensnare leaders. God's plan was never that we would use our influence to control people but rather that we use it to empower people. His plan was not that we seek to rule over people like a dictator, but that we seek to use our influence to help others enter into a place of freedom so that they can experience the joy of a life-giving encounter with Jesus.

In this chapter, we will look at how we can best steward the influence we have, recognising that we have not been given influence to make us greater, but so we can bring glory to the name of Jesus.

## 1. Influence is a gift from God

### i. Thank God for the influence he has given you.

God has given you influence, and that it is your privilege, as His child, to walk in that influence. Without God and His grace in our lives, we would not experience many of the opportunities we have to influence the lives of others.

It is my experience that, sadly, some leaders who move into spheres of influence easily forget the role God has played in opening a way for them to have influence. As a result, their focus seems to shift to their influence rather than to God, who gave them the influence. Inevitably, this leads to God's purposes being diluted and, in some cases, to the leader either losing their position of influence or no longer walking in line with their heavenly Father.

Always remain focused on God and give Him praise for allowing you to walk in the place of influence.

## ii. Seek God as how you walk with His wisdom in the place of influence.

Proverbs 2:6 tells us, "For the Lord gives wisdom; from His mouth come knowledge and understanding."

It is good to acknowledge that wisdom comes from the Lord. Without His wisdom, I do not believe we can walk in the places of influence that He wishes to open up to us. As a result, you need to come before the Lord each day and ask Him for His wisdom. When you do, you are a good steward of the influence God has given you. His wisdom will not only help you walk in the place of influence but will cause you to have something that brings transformation. When you speak from heaven's reserve of wisdom, you can be assured that you always have something wise to say. When you try to use your strength, the influence you have will be short-lived and the impact you achieve will be limited.

Perhaps, like me, there have been times when you have had opportunities to speak into situations and circumstances but had no idea of what to say. In these circumstances, it is good to know that the Bible says, "But if any of you lacks wisdom, let him ask of God, who gives to all generously and without reproach, and it will be given to him." *(James 1:5)*

May you always recognise that you can only walk in the place of influence if you walk in God's wisdom.

### iii. Honour God in all that you do with the influence he has given you.

What influence has God given you? Take a moment to think about all those people you have influence over. They may be your family, friends, church, business, sports team or community. Whoever they are, I believe that God can give you many opportunities to have a positive influence.

I believe God is increasingly placing His sons and daughters in areas where they can bring the influence of heaven in these days. That means each of us has a responsibility to honour God in all of the places of influences that he brings us into.

I have several Christian friends who are politicians who seek to bring the influence of heaven into the political world. At times their influence may not bring about the policies we would like to see, but it allows the light of Jesus to shine in the corridors of power.

Regardless of the level at which we currently live and lead, may we always seek to honour God in all that we do with the influence that he has given to us.

### iv. Take every opportunity to speak the name of Jesus.

Growing up in what was a Christian culture, it was common to hear teachers in school and leaders in public speak about the name of Jesus. Sadly, over the years, this has become less common as secularisation has crept into the nations and people are told they cannot speak the name of Jesus, lest they offend someone.

A war is waging in the heavens! The enemy knows that at the name of Jesus, every knee must bow; he knows that at the name of Jesus, every demon has to flee. And he knows that at the name of Jesus, every deceitful plan he has sought to bring to pass fails. Is it any wonder that the enemy does not want the name of Jesus to be spoken?

As a result, I believe that we, who live and lead like Jesus, need to speak the name of Jesus at every opportunity. We need to declare His name in our homes, workplaces, communities and churches. We need to take every opportunity to speak that name. As you seek to do so, I believe the works of the enemy will be defeated and that for those who lift up the name of Jesus, God will continue to raise them up into greater positions of influence so the name of His Son might be glorified.

## 2. Influence is a gift to others

If you believe that influence is all about you, then you will fail to steward the influence that God has given you. The reality is that influence is given to you by God as a gift for others. By giving you influence, God enables you to have the opportunity to see His Kingdom come in places where, perhaps, God's kingdom has never been seen before.

### i. Influence gives you a voice that others do not have.

In the positions of influence you hold and the places of influence you walk, you will have an opportunity for your voice to be heard where other voices cannot. God gives each of us divine access to be able to speak into positions of power, not so that we can become puffed up, but so that we can speak up for those who have no voice.

I believe God is bringing to pass the verses in Proverbs 31: 8-9 that says, "Speak up for those who cannot speak for themselves, for the rights of all who are destitute. Speak up and judge fairly; defend the rights of the poor and needy."

This, I believe, is the ministry of influence that God has called us to; to speak up for those who cannot speak up for themselves. May we take every opportunity to do so.

### ii. Influence enables you to advocate for others.

The dictionary defines an advocate as a person who publicly supports or recommends a particular cause or policy or a person who puts a case on someone else's behalf. They are a person who influences, defends and protect others.

You cannot be an advocate, however, if you do not have a position of influence. Consequently, I believe that God is going to open up an effective door of opportunity (or influence) for many of His sons and daughters so that they can advocate for others. Already, we are seeing many great ministries arise around the world seeking to advocate on behalf of those who have no voice, for example, victims of trafficking and abuse.

Being an advocate is a ministry that we should be honoured to be part of as it reflects the ministry of Jesus as He advocates for us before the Father. As we advocate for others, I believe God will strengthen us and open up opportunities for us to bring captives into freedom.

### iii. Influence enables you to enhance the lives of people, organisations, communities and nations.

Influence can be used for good reasons or bad. In history, and sadly even today, we do not have to think too long before we can think of people who have, or are, using their influence for evil rather than good. But we are not of those who have evil in their hearts!

You have within your heart the Spirit of Almighty God that enables you to enhance the lives of people, organisations, communities and nations for good. Your sphere of influence right now may be quite small, but I believe that as you steward the gift of influence that God has given you to enhance the lives of others, He will bring you into greater circles of influence. As a result, the influence of His Kingdom will spread across the whole of the earth.

Wherever you live and work right now, continue to seek God as to how you can enhance the lives of those with whom you live or work.

### iv. Influence allows you to see God's Kingdom come.

When Jesus taught His disciples in Matthew 6, he taught them to pray, "Your kingdom come, your will be done, on earth as it is in heaven." Many theologians and others have explained what they believe it means to see God's Kingdom come 'on earth as it is in heaven'. I believe one way we can see His kingdom come is for us to see life on earth come as close as possible to how it is in heaven. That can manifest itself in so many ways, including seeing God's peace, love and healing break out in communities that have not known His presence.

The place of influence that God takes you to is a place where He will enable you to see His Kingdom come on earth as it is in heaven. Why? Because each of us who live and lead like Jesus carries within us the DNA and presence of heaven itself. We have already been seated with Christ in heavenly places and it is from there that we have been given authority by God to walk in influence so that we might be able to see His Kingdom come.

## 3. Stewarding Influence God's way

Finally, in this chapter, I want to consider what it means for you to steward influence God's way. In the natural, every person of influence has a responsibility to steward their influence responsibly. The children of God, however, have a greater responsibility to steward their influence as they recognise it has been given to them by God for His purposes not theirs.

In particular, I believe to steward influence God's ways:

### i. Your focus must remain on Jesus.

What are you doing each day to ensure that your focus remains on Jesus?

The longer we live and lead, the busier life can get. As we get busier, the spiritual disciplines that are foundational to our faith can begin to slip. It is often not intentional, it just happens and before we know it, our focus has become on the position that we hold rather than on Jesus.

Commit to set aside time each day to rest in God's presence, read the Bible, pray and worship the one who is worthy of praise. When you do, you will be able to remain focused on Jesus, and the impact of your influence will be greater.

### ii. Your life, both privately and in publicly, is aligned with the Bible.

Holiness is not a popular subject nowadays. Many of our forefathers in the faith believed that holiness was an essential part of their Christian life and witness. My grandmother used to say that 'holiness is next to godliness'.

While some of the holiness movement people became more focused on the works of holiness than the God who is Holy, I believe that we need to seek to ensure that our private and public lives align with the Bible. God has opened positions of influence to us, and these positions often place us in the public spotlight in ways that we may not have thought. As a result, we must do all we can to live uprightly before God and before man so that our lives can continue to bring glory to the name of Jesus.

### iii. Your heart is aligned with God's desires, not your desires.

Jeremiah, the Old Testament prophet, talks about the evil desires of the heart. The unrepentant heart is indeed evil. As redeemed a redeemed child of God, however, your heart has been cleansed by the blood of Jesus. That said, you need to be aware that the enemy will seek to sow into your heart's desires that do not align with God's. If the enemy cannot stop you from walking in a place of influence, he will want to corrupt you so that you cannot be impactful in that place of influence.

Hence, we need to be aware that the place of influence is a place where we will often be tempted. As a result, we need to constantly check that our desires are aligned with God's desires. A key part of ensuring this requires you shutting every possible door through which the enemy would seek to bring his plans to pass.

### iv. Your delight is in the praise of God, not in the applause of man.

Finally, I believe we can steward the influence that God has given us effectively when we desire to praise God and to walk in His blessing rather than the applause of man. We do not want to follow the footsteps of those who fell into the trap of the flattery of man but we want to be those who seek to hear God say 'well done good and faithful servant'.

## Prayer

*Father, we are forever grateful that we are your sons and daughters and that you have blessed us with the opportunity to walk in places and positions of influence. We dedicate our hearts afresh to you and ask that you, by the power of the Holy Spirit, would help us walk in wisdom and integrity, so that in all we do, the name of Jesus might be glorified and we might see your Kingdom come on earth as it is in heaven. Amen.*

*You have the ability to speak into the lives of many people and help them see the potential that God has placed within them.*

## Chapter 12
# Maximising Influence

If our influence is restricted to the here and now and does not go beyond our current context and generation, that is good. But how much better would it be if our influence were to bring transformational change beyond our context and lifetime?

I believe God has given you and I influence that he wants to transcend our current context and our current generation. He wants you to be intentional in how you invite others into the knowledge and wisdom that He has imparted to you so they can have an accelerated pathway to greater impact and influence.

The life of learning that we have journeyed on has taught us many lessons that younger people need to learn. I have sadly known many leaders who have taken their lifetime of wisdom and knowledge with them to their grave. How much better it would be to create a legacy plan that enables you to take what you have learned and share it beyond your current sphere of influence.

### Who have you the capacity to influence?

Through the gift of influence, I believe that God has opened up opportunities for everyone who lives and leads like Jesus to influence multitudes of people, some whom we know and some we don't know.

Our sphere of influence is both present and future and includes those:

- We influence today as a result of how they see us live and lead.
- Who influence today as result of how they are impacted by our example.
- We influence today, beyond our immediate context, through media
- Who will be an influence tomorrow as a result of what they learn from our leadership and legacy.

## How can we maximise influence?

Having lived and led like Jesus through seasons of trial and triumph and been given influence by God, we have an opportunity to begin developing a legacy from the influence He has given us. You will be familiar with the word 'legacy' in the context of leaving money, property or personal belongings in a will. But I want you to consider what you can leave for those coming after you who will live and lead like Jesus.

Here are some suggestions of what you can do to create a legacy for those who will follow you:

## 1. Invest

If you are or have been in business, you will be familiar with the concept of investing. You may well have invested in stocks and shares or human or capital resources. In the same way, I believe you can invest now in developing people who will lead and live like Jesus in years to come. In the list that follows, I will consider practical ways that you can do so. You may be in a position where you sense God asking you to set aside money to invest in others. He may even be prompting you to develop or expand a trust fund that empowers the development of young leaders. Regardless of what He is saying, I would encourage you to follow His leading. Your investment in Kingdom leaders will bring a Kingdom return to you and your family.

## 2. Mine

The word 'mine' may seem out of context here; however, I am not referring to mining for gold or valuable resources in a natural sense but helping others identify the gold that God has placed in them. People in your circle of influence will often not have the ability to see the gold that God has placed within them. They need help to identify it and bring it to the surface.

As a person of influence, I believe you have the ability to speak into the lives of many people and help them see the potential that God has placed within them. You can help them become all that God has placed within them. Even when your influence has waned, they will be able to live life to the fullness of the potential God has placed within them, creating a Kingdom impact that goes beyond the time and place where you live and lead.

## 3. Coach

American leaders will be very familiar with the term 'coach' from a sporting context. The Cambridge dictionary defines a coach as 'someone whose job is to teach people to improve at a sport, skill, or school subject'.[9]

As Jesus-centred leaders, we have a God-given opportunity to use our influence to coach other people to do what they cannot. We can instil in them the belief that they can do what they think they cannot, and we can impart to them the skills that will enable them to excel at what they do. In doing so, we are creating a legacy where we use the gifts and talents God gave us to release abilities in the generations that follow after us. As a coach, you are not only able to pass on skills to help people do things better, you can coach them in how to live and work more like Jesus. Now that's a legacy of influence that I'm sure we all would like to have!

## 4. Mentor

In community, business and church circles there can be confusion as to the difference between a coach and a mentor. A coach primarily teaches someone how to do something, whereas a mentor, as defined by the Cambridge dictionary, is a 'person who gives a younger or less experienced person help and advice over a period of time, especially at work or school'.[10]

Within our sphere of present and future influence, as set out earlier in this chapter, we can mentor people through help and advice, over time, in how they can live and lead like Jesus. Perhaps you have had a mentor, someone you connect with from time to time, who can offer you

---

[9] https://dictionary.cambridge.org/dictionary/english/coach

[10] https://dictionary.cambridge.org/dictionary/english/mentor

God-inspired help and advice. Currently, I have a few people I would regard as mentors. They are somewhat older and more experienced than me and have prophetic insight that allows them to speak wise words into my life.

Who are you mentoring? Could you begin to mentor two or three people a month? It could be as simple as a monthly Zoom call or meeting for a coffee. God has given you and I the ability to mentor people so they receive a legacy from the wisdom that God has imparted to us.

## 5. Jethro Walks

Many of you may not be familiar with the concept of 'Jethro Walks', but you will be familiar with the name Jethro and will know he was the father-in-law of Moses. In Exodus 18, we read that Jethro drew alongside his son-in-law, the younger leader, and offered advice on how to lead the people and avoid burnout. The advice he gave is something many could still benefit from today.

So, what is a Jethro Walk? Recently, a retired Christian businessman, who had begun to meet a few younger leaders each month and join them for a walk along the beach, approached me. He described it as an opportunity to walk with them, let them talk about their concerns and offer them advice on how they might proceed. It was nothing formal and certainly less intensive than coaching or mentoring.

Having listened to my friend's desire to walk alongside more leaders and having identified some other people with a similar passion, I felt God drop into my spirit two words 'Jethro Walks'. I wonder could you begin doing some Jethro Walks? It is as simple as taking a walk with a younger leader, allowing them to share their concerns and offering them godly advice.

## 6. Wisdom Downloads

Within you and I, those whom God has called to live, lead and have an influence on others, lies wisdom gained from a lifetime of experience and downloads we have received from our heavenly Father. Over many years, we have walked in the blessing of knowing that if any man lacks wisdom, he can ask the Father for that. *(James 1:5)*

Across the world today, I believe there are millions of men and women of God who have lived and led with integrity for decades. In doing so, they have a living well of wisdom within them that was not just designed to be used in their time and place but to be 'downloaded' for generations yet to come.

In 2016, a local Christian businessman approached me and asked how he and a friend could download the wisdom that God had given to them over 50-plus years in business and church leadership. That request sparked the idea in me of creating a podcast called the 'Wisdom Download' in which established leaders, perhaps like you, download the wisdom that God has placed within them in an interview format. These thoughts are revealed with others online so that it can be shared with younger and emerging leaders in years to come.

Make plans to 'download' the wisdom God has given you.

## 7. Writing

At school, I loved maths and hated English. I planned on being an accountant as I thought that was the career for someone who liked maths. However, I failed to get into an accountancy degree and ended up doing a degree in economics. Imagine my horror in finding out that the final exams involved 15 hours of written exams. I hated writing!

You might find this revelation somewhat strange considering you are now nearing the end of reading a book that I have written! I find it strange, too, but I know God has been calling me to write for many years. I kept putting it off as I thought I was too busy, I hated writing and I needed a lot of help with proofreading what I write!

You might find this revelation somewhat strange, considering you are now nearing the end of reading a book that I have written! I find it strange, but I know God has been calling me to write for many years. I kept putting it off as I thought I was too busy; I hated writing, and I needed a lot of help with proofreading what I write!

## 8. Podcasting

A final and very much 21st Century way of maximising your influence is to begin to create podcasts. Through these, you communicate life and leadership principles with those in your immediate sphere of influence and people across the world. Your podcasts will be available through the wide range of podcast streaming services that now exist.

If you want to use your influence to share insights and wisdom with younger leaders, you need to learn how to share that wisdom in smaller bite-sized segments and use graphics to illustrate what you are saying. Millennials and the generations that are following them are said to have shorter attention spans but tend to have a greater capacity to consume information.

If you say that you do not have the skills to create a podcast, well, neither do I, but I didn't let that stop me, and neither should you. Many online services enable you to produce good quality podcasts for relatively little money.

Use every means possible to maximise the influence God has given you here and now and in the years that come.

## And finally...

Take some time to answer these questions and, in doing so, I believe you will be making a conscientious decision to not only live and lead like Jesus today but to allow the influence you have now to help others live and lead like Jesus in years to come.

1. What wisdom and insights have you gained from living and leading like Jesus?

2. What wisdom has God downloaded to you over the years?

3. How are you currently recording and cataloguing that wisdom?

4. What steps can you take now and in the future to maximise the influence God has given you?

5. What steps will you take today to begin imparting insight and wisdom to others?

## A final prayer

*Father, we are thankful that you love us and have enabled us to live and lead like Jesus. We thank you for our identity in Christ and the gifts that you have imparted to us that allow us to live and lead through the power of the Holy Spirit. We are grateful that you continue to give us inspiration and wisdom to live and lead in a manner that honours you. As we continue to walk closely with you, we ask that you help us to have a greater impact in all that we do, so that we might see your Kingdom come on earth as it is in heaven. We thank you for the influence you have given us and we ask that you help us steward it well and maximise our influence by imparting the insights and wisdom you have given us to others. In Jesus's name,*

*Amen!*

TOMMY STEWART

# About the Author

Tommy Stewart has been active in leadership within the private, public and voluntary sector for more than 30 years. He is married to Roberta and has three adult sons: Simon, Daniel and Thomas. The family lives in Northern Ireland, where Tommy and Roberta help to lead Mid Antrim Vineyard.

After spending 15 years managing Christian organisations, employability programmes and local authority services, Tommy launched a consultancy company in 2002 that provided research, strategy development and evaluation services, for public, private and voluntary sector organisations.

Since 2016 he has been solely focused on consultancy and leadership support for churches and missional organisations in the UK, Ireland and around in many other nations. Tommy serves as a trustee of local, regional and international Christian organisations including Youth for Christ, Bible Society and Arrow Leadership.

Tommy holds a Master's degree in Missional Leadership, a Bachelor of Arts degree in Theology, and a Bachelor of Science degree in Economics, along with Post Graduate Diplomas in Management and Pastoral Leadership.

TOMMY STEWART

# Let me help you

It is my desire to help each of you live and lead like Jesus and, as a result, I would love to invite you to join the 'Live and Lead Like Jesus' community at:

www.liveandleadlikejesus.com

Community members have direct access to practical tools and resources based upon the four main thematic of the book: Identity, Inspiration, Impact and Influence.

Let's continue our journey together.

Your friend,

Tommy

Printed in Great Britain
by Amazon